The Recycling, Use, and Repair of Tools

The Recycling, Use, and Repair of Tools

ALEXANDER G. WEYGERS

Illustrated by the author

 VAN NOSTRAND REINHOLD COMPANY
New York   Cincinnati   Toronto   London   Melbourne

BY THE SAME AUTHOR

THE MODERN BLACKSMITH
THE MAKING OF TOOLS

Copyright © 1978 by Litton Educational Publishing, Inc.
Library of Congress Catalog Card Number 78-17188
ISBN 0-442-29358-5 (ppr.)
ISBN 0-442-29357-7 (cloth)

Printed in U.S.A.

Illustrations by Alexander G. Weygers
Photos by Peter Hopkins
Illustrations for Chapters 7 and 27 from *The Making of Tools,*
by Alexander G. Weygers.

Published in 1978 by Van Nostrand Reinhold Company
A division of Litton Educational Publishing, Inc.
135 West 50th Street, New York, NY 10020, U.S.A.

Van Nostrand Reinhold Limited
1410 Birchmount Road
Scarborough, Ontario M1P 2E7, Canada

Van Nostrand Reinhold Australia Pty. Ltd.
17 Queen Street
Mitcham, Victoria 3132, Australia

Van Nostrand Reinhold Company Limited
Molly Millars Lane
Wokingham, Berkshire, England

16 15 14 13 12 11 10 9 8 7 6 5 4 3 2 1

Library of Congress Cataloging in Publication Data

Weygers, Alexander G
    The recycling, use, and repair of tools.

    1. Metal-work. 2. Woodwork. 3. Tools. I. Title.
TT213.W48   621.9'08   78-17188
ISBN 0-442-29357-7
ISBN 0-442-29358-5 pbk.

Contents

Introduction

The scrap steel yards across the country are full of every conceivable metal object discarded for reasons of wear, obsolescence, or damage. Much of this material can become useful stock for the beginner, as well as the skilled metal craftsman, who intends to "make do" with what can be gleaned from this so-called junk.

Those who must fabricate items that can be made only from new bar and plate steel if they are to compete in the commercial market cannot afford to spend the time it takes to work with salvaged odds and ends. They will help to feed the scrap pile instead of being fed by it.

I have for many years practiced and enjoyed making something out of nothing in constructing a tool or reconditioning a junked piece of machinery. My aim in writing this book has been to compile information on how to do just that for the person with a combination machine shop and smithy.

It is through actual demonstration, seeing how to manipulate tools to make tools, that I believe the student benefits most. But short of that one can learn from books in which the illustrations come as near as possible to live demonstrations. I have tried to present the information in such a way that the reader can imagine he is watching me making things in the shop.

That approach has been put to the test in my previous books, *The Making of Tools* and *The Modern Blacksmith.* Since their publication a few years ago, readers have reported results that underscore my conviction that the same guidelines to self-teaching should be continued here. I have done this in the hope that it will be possible for those who diligently follow these instructions to advance and round out their know-how with this extended information.

If a self-employed and independent smith can be a good machinist as well, there is great promise that in time his abilities will prove to be a better security than any money in the bank.

1. How to Repair Broken Garden Tools

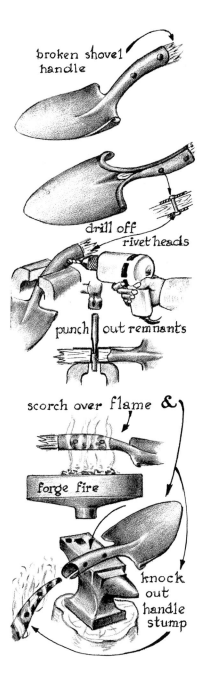

broken shovel handle

drill off rivet heads

punch out remnants

scorch over flame &

forge fire

knock out handle stump

Most long-handled garden tools break where the wooden handle enters the steel part of the tool. Not knowing how to replace a handle, most people throw the whole tool away and buy a new one. Their loss is our gain if we like to recycle waste, have a modest shop to make such repairs, and have the time to do it.

Removing the Handle Remnant from the Shovel Blade Socket

The wooden stub is held in the socket by two rivets. Clamp the socket in the vise as illustrated, showing the countersunk depression in the socket. With a 3/8-inch drill, or similar sized tool appropriate to the task, clear the depression of the rivet head. Next, straddle the rivet location over the partially opened vise and punch out the rivet remnant. The handle stub can now be knocked out. If this proves too difficult to do, heat the shovel socket over a flame until the wood begins to scorch. The stub can then easily be released and the new handle installed.

Installing the New Handle

If you live near an orchard, the farmer may let you have a branch from his fruitwood prunings. Choose a fairly straight one, thick enough to make two handles. Saw the branch in half lengthwise. After trimming, each handle cross section will be oblong, which will do just as well as handles that have round cross sections. In selecting the branch, try also to pick one with a natural curve ending that approximates the curve in the shovel blade socket. Shape the end to fit the curve closely.

Heat the handle socket to the point of scorching the wood, then quickly clamp the shovel in the vise and hammer the handle home. If you do not succeed on the first try because the handle does not match the socket curve well enough, you may have to preheat the end before hammering it into place. You can easily accomplish this heating (not shown) by dipping the curved end in water and holding it in the flame until the water has evaporated and wood begins to scorch. Repeat this operation maybe four or five times. Between the steam of the evaporating water and the heat of the fire, the entire curved end becomes heated to the core, momentarily making the wood limp. At the same time the handle socket should be heated to the point of scorching wood. Then quickly clamp the blade in the vise and hammer the limp handle into the socket. It will easily follow the curvature of the socket under the hammerblows on the other end of the handle. Following the curvature of the socket, the limp end flexes as if it were made of rubber.

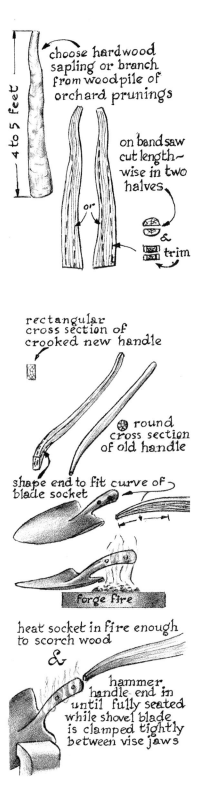

choose hardwood sapling or branch from woodpile of orchard prunings

4 to 5 feet

on bandsaw cut length-wise in two halves.

or

& trim

rectangular cross section of crooked new handle

round cross section of old handle

shape end to fit curve of blade socket

forge fire

heat socket in fire enough to scorch wood

&

hammer handle end in until fully seated while shovel blade is clamped tightly between vise jaws

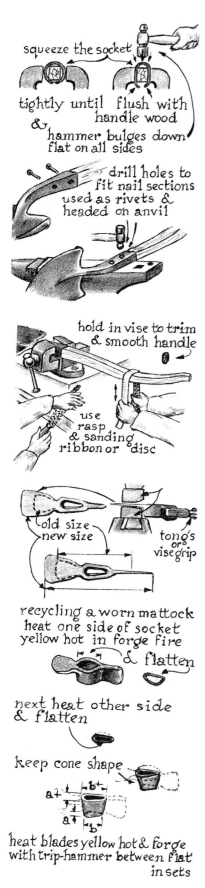

squeeze the socket
tightly until flush with handle wood & hammer bulges down flat on all sides

drill holes to fit nail sections used as rivets & headed on anvil

hold in vise to trim & smooth handle

use rasp & sanding ribbon or disc

old size / new size

tongs or vise grip

recycling a worn mattock heat one side of socket yellow hot in forge fire & flatten

next heat other side & flatten

keep cone shape

a+ +b+
a+ +b+

heat blades yellow hot & forge with trip-hammer between flat insets

Let all cool off before taking the next step.

With the handle firmly seated, clamp the socket between the vise jaws until the steel sides of the socket press firmly onto the wood.

Since the shovel socket is round and the new handle cross section is oblong, the socket must be reshaped to hold the handle. Squeeze the socket onto the handle between the vise jaws as forcefully as possible. Hammer the bulging upper part of the socket flush with the flat part of the handle.

After the bulges on all four sides of the socket have been hammered down flat in this way, drill holes through the wood from both sides, meeting halfway to secure alignment. Choose a nail to fit the hole and clip off pieces to be used as rivets. Hammer them through the holes and, with the heads placed flush on the anvil facing, rivet them with a lightweight ball peen hammer.

Round off all sharp edges on the handle with rasps, abrasive ribbons, or small, rubber-backed disc sanders rotating in a hand-held electric drill.

I have used for years several shovels that have been recycled in this way. I enjoy their extra-long, slightly curved handles, which seem to lighten the work when I need to twist the shovel in levering action.

RECYCLING AN OLD WORN MATTOCK

Continued resharpening of the blades will in due time shorten them to the point that the mattock will no longer do what it was designed to do. All the same, the steel closest to the handle socket will remain thick enough to be peened out longer in the forge. This restores a blade long enough to make the tool useful once more.

Lengthening and Widening Both Blades

Although hand-peening the blades is not too big a job, you can do it in a fraction of the time with the regular flat-faced insets of a trip-hammer. This not only saves your back, but improves the steel's quality as well, because trip-hammer blows can be forceful enough to *pack* the steel most effectively.

Since this process makes the tool a lighter gauge than the original one, the old handle will be too large and clumsy. To narrow the opening for a lighter handle, follow the illustrations as guidelines. They show that the length of the socket hole itself will not change if one side is forged at a time and the other side remains cold (but not brittle). Hammering the hot side compacts the steel in an upsetting action. In this way, the handle socket becomes narrower, but not longer, than it was originally. The new, more slender handle will be strong enough for the more slender head.

Dressing the Blank and Hardening the Blade Edges

As always with tools of this size, the hard, coarse, and large motor-driven grinding wheel will do the best job of dressing.

Hardening the tool blade edges is somewhat simpler if (as with a mattock) both edges are far enough apart that heating one edge will not anneal the other.

Place one blade in the fire over a slow heat and bring the edge to a *cherry red*. Allow that heat to dissipate up to the handle socket. At this point, quench the whole blank in oil. Treat the other edge in the same way.

You will end up with a new, though recycled, mattock that will stand up under normal use for several years before it has worn to the point where rehardening is necessary.

grind blade ends sharp, next

heat cherry red one at a time
to → harden ends only

& quench in oil one at a time

Installing the New Handle

Make a mattock handle from a salvaged fruit tree branch (as described in the making of shovel handles, page 9), fashioned into a shape to your own liking. The top of the handle socket, being somewhat larger than the bottom, allows the end of the split handle to be wedged open and seated firmly by filling the entire socket cavity.

This slender, lightweight mattock is a welcome addition to the bulkier, heavyweight ones, and you will find it useful in many different ways.

cut hardwood handle to fit
new socket & cut slot with saw

to take wedge which is $\frac{1}{8}$"
forged from flat stock

after wedge is driven in
drill hole through socket & wedge
for rivet

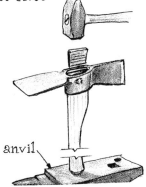

anvil

2. Making a Charcoal Brazier and Screening Scoop

charcoal brazier made from a salvaged truck head light housing & an ash basin from a large hubcap

Using a charcoal brazier to cook food on a picnic table can be very convenient. I have used the brazier described here for many years, on camping trips as well as at home.

In campgrounds where fires have been doused there is usually a quantity of unburned charcoal to be found. The screening scoop is simply used to separate the charcoal from the ashes, and in no time the brazier is full and ready to use. Good charcoal can be scooped from your home fireplace as well.

The brazier bowl is made from a car headlight, the ash basin from a hubcap. To light the fire, place a wad of crumpled paper below the perforated grate in the basin. If the charcoal is dry and the grate holes not too small, the fire should start easily. Let the paper burn completely before fanning the glowing coals with a piece of cardboard to speed up the spread of the flames. There will soon be a steady, smokeless, safe fire giving fifteen to twenty-five minutes of cooking time.

TO MAKE THE BRAZIER

Try to find as large a truck headlight housing as you can in auto wrecking yards. The hubcap to catch the ashes should be larger in diameter than the headlight housing.

If the headlight cooling holes are too small, enlarge them to at least 3/8-inch in diameter. Place them close together to make it easier for the flames from the paper below to ignite the charcoal.

To make the grill over the charcoal fire, drill 5/16-inch holes evenly spaced along the top of the housing to take the 5/16-inch grill rods on both sides. Bend them as shown and lace them through the holes.

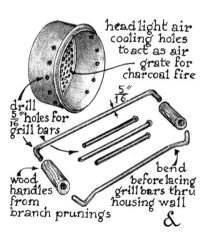

head light air cooling holes to act as air grate for charcoal fire

drill 5/16" holes for grill bars

wood handles from branch prunings

bend before lacing grill bars thru housing wall

&

Assemble the two outer grill rods with wooden handles so that the brazier can be picked up safely while the charcoal is burning.

To install the four legs, follow exactly the instruction in the illustration. Their arrangement creates a self-locking hold between brazier and ash basin, spacing them in a permanent tight fit.

I find that a brazier of this type works as well as, if not better than, those that are made from heavy iron. Constructed from car parts, it weighs only a fraction of most cast-iron braziers.

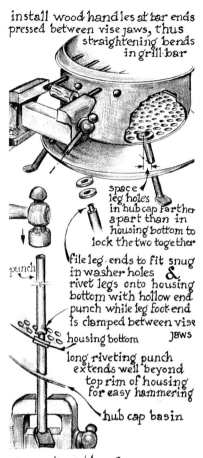

install wood handles at bar ends pressed between vise jaws, thus straightening bends in grill-bar

space leg holes in hub cap farther apart than in housing bottom to lock the two together

file leg ends to fit snug in washer holes & rivet legs onto housing bottom with hollow end punch while leg foot-end is clamped between vise jaws

housing bottom

long riveting punch extends well beyond top rim of housing for easy hammering

hub cap basin

punch

THE CHARCOAL SCOOP

A piece of salvaged galvanized sheet metal that can be cut with tinsnips is easily shaped and folded as illustrated. It acts as a retaining fence while the charcoal is shoveled up. Small remnants of guy wire cable, often thrown away by electrical companies, can be used for the tines of the scoop. Untwist the cable section and hammer each wire straight on the anvil. Curve a mild steel bar slightly, as shown, for the assembly of the tines. About sixteen tines is a suitable number. Drill the holes into which they will fit snugly, then hammer-lock them tight. The hammering actually squeezes the steel bar sections onto the tine endings.

scoop to gather & screen charcoal from campfires or home fire places

retaining fence cut from a scrapped roofing sheet steel panel

fold along lines & flatten edges around end wires & cinch with rubber mallet on anvil

make the tines from scrap guy-wire cable

untwist into &

cold hammer straight on anvil

1/8"

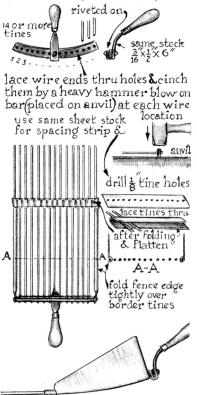

bend a mild steel bar $\frac{3}{16}$" x $\frac{1}{2}$" x 8" & drill the holes $\frac{1}{8}$" dia evenly spaced

14 or more tines

riveted on

same stock $\frac{3}{16}$" x $\frac{1}{2}$" x 6"

1 2 3 . . . .

lace wire ends thru holes & cinch them by a heavy hammer blow on bar (placed on anvil) at each wire location

use same sheet stock for spacing strip &

anvil

drill $\frac{1}{8}$" tine holes

lace tines thru

after folding & flatten

A-A

A   A

fold fence edge tightly over border tines

bend each tine with a slight curve to ease scooping action

Use the same mild steel stock to bend a small handle holder, which serves as a tool tang. Rivet it onto the curved bar. The wooden handle can be burned onto the tang.

Cut a tine spacer strip of the same sheet metal used for the scoop wall. Punch through it evenly spaced small holes like the ones in the steel bar. Fold the metal strip along the row of holes and lace the tines through them.

Once the strip is in the correct position, flatten it over the tines with a rubber hammer, using the anvil facing as a base. The sheet metal strip easily yields under the hammerblows so that it is pressed out between the tines. This locks them in position so they will not obstruct the scooping up of the charcoal, yet the whole assembly is held firmly together.

3. A Candlestick

The round disc cutouts used here were cut from heavy plate steel on a factory milling machine. The plate out of which the discs were cut was used to reinforce a cylinder that was subjected to enormous pressure from within. I was fortunate to come by a great quantity of these waste discs. It proved very much worth my while to make special trip-hammer insets to aid me in making various articles from this excellent scrap material. The base and drip cup of a candlestick were made of these, as decribed in Chapter 26. The candlestick shown here makes use of these discs.

Drill a hole in the center of the large rosette that acts as the base. Tap into it a 1/2-inch thread to take the threaded candlestick column. Thread a similar hole in the drip cup to fit the threaded top of the candlestick.

Make the twist in the column of the candlestick by heating one half of the rod, twisting it, and cooling it. Then heat the other half and twist it counter to the first, giving variety to the design.

Cold forge the candle socket from a section of pipe and thread it to fit the little extra protruding thread in the center of the drip cup.

Mild steel conduit pipe can be cold forged to a remarkable extent, but because these pipes are bonded with a welded seam it is only by compacting that they can be made into cones as shown. Expanding the diameter of the pipe, however, cannot be done by cold stretching. Hammering the pipe ending over a cone would only break the weld. A very small amount of stretching can be done by hammering the end *very carefully* over a bick or an anvil horn in a peening action.

If you are lucky enough to find on a scrap pile some seamless tubing, it can be stretched outward by force to a certain extent without peening. The illustrations clarify this further.

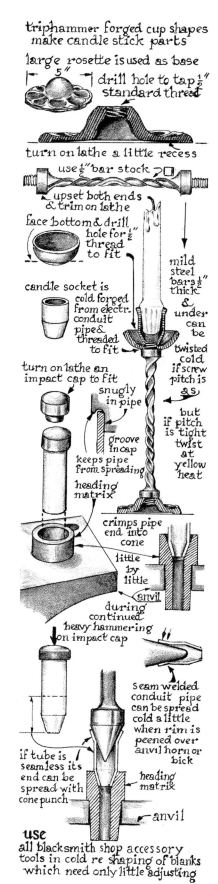

triphammer forged cup shapes make candle stick parts

large rosette is used as base

5" drill hole to tap ½" standard thread

turn on lathe a little recess

use ½" bar stock

upset both ends & trim on lathe

face bottom & drill hole for ½" thread to fit

candle socket is cold forged from electr. conduit pipe & threaded to fit

mild steel bars ½" thick & under can be twisted cold if screw pitch is as)

but if pitch is tight twist at yellow heat

turn on lathe an impact cap to fit snugly in pipe

groove in cap keeps pipe from spreading

heading matrix

crimps pipe end into cone

little by little

anvil

during continued heavy hammering on impact cap

seam welded conduit pipe can be spread cold a little when rim is peened over anvil horn or bick

if tube is seamless its end can be spread with cone punch

heading matrix

anvil

use
all blacksmith shop accessory tools in cold re shaping of blanks which need only little adjusting

4. Making Tool Handle Ferrules and Shoulders

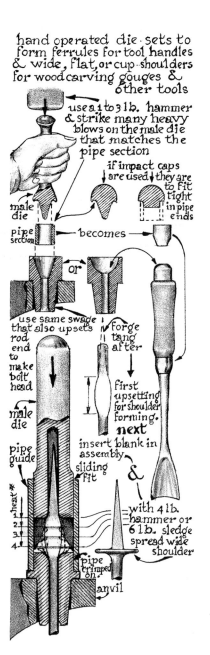

hand operated die sets to form ferrules for tool handles & wide, flat, or cup shoulders for woodcarving gouges & other tools

use a 1 to 3 lb. hammer & strike many heavy blows on the male die that matches the pipe section

if impact caps are used they are to fit tight in pipe ends

male die

pipe section

becomes

or

use same swage that also upsets rod end to make bolt head

male die

pipe guide

heat *
1
2
3
4

forge tang after

first upsetting for shoulder forming. **next** insert blank in assembly

sliding fit

&

with 4 lb. hammer or 6 lb. sledge spread wide shoulder

pipe crimped on.

anvil

Tool handle ferrules are made in the same way as the candle sockets described in Chapter 3. The only difference is that many tool handles do need to have the small diameter cone endings if tool shoulders are fairly small.

MAKING A JIG FOR STRAIGHT FERRULES

Straight ferrules without cone endings are required for tools with large diameter shoulders. Attempts to make such wide shoulders without a jig will prove to be not only very frustrating, but time-consuming as well. Thus it will be worthwhile to construct a jig, as shown in the illustrations.

Error during the upsetting of the rod to make the shoulder will require constant straightening up of the bends that are formed. The jig prevents this by acting as a guide during hammering and makes it possible to correctly distribute the upset rod section. Once any danger of bending has been eliminated, the male part of the die can be hammered down with a heavy sledgehammer to spread the shoulder enough to take a wide diameter ferrule.

TOOL SHOULDERS

The combination of ferrule and shoulder in one forging gives the handle a streamlined look but does not necessarily make it any more functional. The tool serves just as well if it has only a very small shoulder pressed onto a tight-fitting heavy washer, which in turn reaches the rim of a ferrule that has been pressed on the wood of the handle. So it is up to the craftsman who makes his own tools if he wants to spend extra time and effort simply to make his tool more attractive with such a combination of shoulder and cup washer. Shoulders can also be formed into cup shapes in a set of hand dies made for that purpose.

Once the jig has been made for the wide shoulders and ferrule cups, making the whole tool would not take much longer. It is making the jig, not making the tool itself, that takes the time.

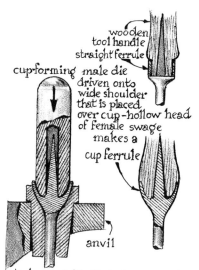

wooden tool handle
straight ferrule
cup-forming male die driven onto wide shoulder that is placed over cup-hollow head of female swage makes a cup ferrule
anvil

stock must fit die hole accurately without binding. During forging cup shoulder is formed yellow hot while hammered in place.

5. A Pump to Recycle Waste Water

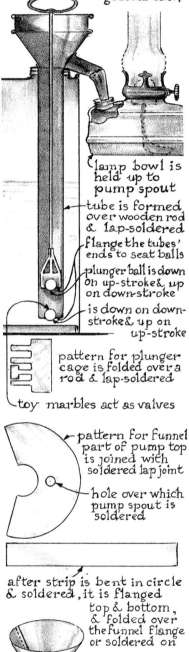

pump to fill lamps with kerosene from standard gallon can.

lamp bowl is held up to pump spout

tube is formed over wooden rod & lap-soldered

flange the tubes' ends to seat balls

plunger ball is down on up-stroke & up on down-stroke

is down on down-stroke & up on up-stroke

pattern for plunger cage is folded over a rod & lap-soldered

toy marbles act as valves

pattern for funnel part of pump top is joined with soldered lap joint

hole over which pump spout is soldered

after strip is bent in circle & soldered, it is flanged top & bottom, & folded over the funnel flange or soldered on

spout pattern is folded & bent, soldered at elbow & flanged at base to fit onto funnel & soldered to it

To make such a pump I followed a very simple design used throughout the Orient, where people pump kerosene from a five-gallon can into the little lamps they use every night.

It was in Java, Indonesia, that I saw such a little pump made before my own eyes. In the marketplace the tinsmith soldered together the various parts he had cut out with tinsnips from flattened five-gallon cans. None of the moving parts had been machined or put together in a machine-precisioned way.

The pumping is done by quick, short up-and-down movements of the plunger. There is some backflow leaking between the plunger and the cylinder, but it somehow does not reduce the pump's effectiveness. The liquid rises quickly to fill the open top part of the pump body so that the kerosene gently flows by gravity through the small spout into the lamp bowl.

It is this design, as I adapted it, that we are now following in the making of a larger pump to recycle waste water during a drought year.

It must be remembered that each person wishing to make such a pump must do it from the odds and ends he has accumulated and that his supply is bound to differ from mine. The final appearance of his product, therefore, will probably be quite unlike the one I am showing here.

First note that the waste water from the bathroom tub and washbowl is collected in a fifty-gallon drum. The idea is to pump the water high up into some kind of a holding tank (38) and to make a bottom valve arrangement (6–7) to hold the column of water above it—without leaking, if possible. In this way the water can flow by gravity out of the holding tank for as long as it takes the hose to distribute the water.

Place the top holding tank a few feet *above* the garden level so the water will flow easily to it by gravity. Hand-pumping from time to time will distribute the water, saving on the use of electric energy at the same time.

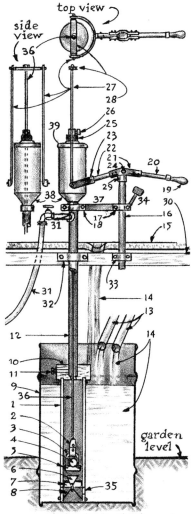

pump is to distribute rain & waste water to garden

1 pump body is made of waste plastic drainpipe material
2 copper link–3 copper wire cage–4 rubber ball valve
5 copper valve seat–6 rubber valve–7 copper valve seat
8 rubber band–9 waterdrum
10 wooden coupling–11 set screw
12 electrical conduit pipe
13 plastic drainpipe–14 water
15 outdoor porch–16,17,18 clamps & brace–19 pump handle
20 handle bar–21 yoke–22-23 fork arm of handle bar
24 yoke hinge pin
25 rubber buffer–26 collar–
27 two linkage rods–28 yoke
29 hinge body–30 porch timber
31 garden hose take-off & bib
32 installation clamps–33 rain water from porch–34 rubber stop for pump handle
35 intake holes–plunger rod
37 brace   36
38 holding tank & lid 39

SELECTING THE MATERIAL FOR THE PUMP

Sections of ABS plastic drainpipes can often be found on house construction site scrap piles. This salvaged section was 4 inches in diameter.

The storage can is a fifty-gallon oil drum, often discarded or available at minimum cost in scrap yards. Coat it on the inside with hot roofing tar to make it rustproof.

Large diameter electrical conduit pipe is available from wrecking yards at very little cost or from heaps of waste thrown out during reconstruction of old buildings.

The three-gallon tank at the top happened to be on my own scrap pile. It was originally used in a milk separator machine. Anything else—a galvanized drum or small garbage can, for instance—would do.

The main pump rod (36) and linkage rods (27) are made from an unreeled coilspring heated at yellow heat and straightened (as described in my book *The Modern Blacksmith*). Hammer it out straight and remember that spring steel, even in an annealed state, remains resilient.

Large strips of steel are forged or bent into brackets or braces that can be anchored against a part of a building to brace the pump assembly spaced from the handle column in a clamping action.

All in all, the various small details shown in the illustration are likely to be accumulated, in one form or another, by most of us when gathering scrap steel, and especially by those who have geared their activities to such shop practices.

Once you have assembled the elements needed for this type of pump arrangement, begin with the major element.

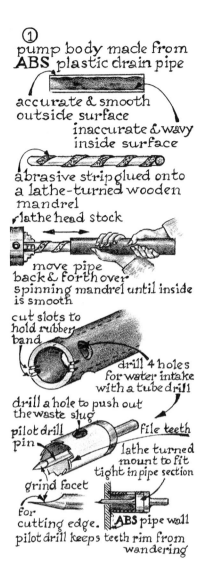

① pump body made from
ABS plastic drain pipe

accurate & smooth
outside surface

inaccurate & wavy
inside surface

abrasive strip glued onto
a lathe-turned wooden
mandrel

lathe head stock

move pipe
back & forth over
spinning mandrel until inside
is smooth

cut slots to
hold rubber
band

drill 4 holes
for water intake
with a tube drill

drill a hole to push out
the waste slug

pilot drill
pin

file teeth

lathe turned
mount to fit
tight in pipe section

grind facet

for
cutting edge.   **ABS** pipe wall
pilot drill keeps teeth rim from
wandering

THE PUMP BODY

The plastic pipe section I used proved to be smooth on the outside but not on the inside. Should this happen to be so in your case and should you have no other choice, you can make the inside accurate as shown in the illustrations.

First turn a wooden mandrel on the wood lathe. Glue onto it a cloth strip of coarse abrasive. It should barely fit the inside diameter of the pipe section. With the mandrel clamped in the lathe chuck, rotate it at normal speed. Slip the pipe section back and forth over the full length of this abrasive core. The pipe interior will thus be smoothed out.

THE INTAKE VALVE

It is here that you must apply some ingenuity to make do with the material that you have. My own decision was to let the total pump assembly rest upon the bottom of the fifty-gallon drum. This called for drilling intake holes 1 inch from the rim of the pipe bottom to allow the water to enter the pump chamber and placing the bottom valve just above them. I used a rubber toilet ball (6) for the bottom valve. To it I attached a strip of copper ending in a hook. I attached a rubber band to the hook to hold the ball down for a good seating. Each end of the rubber band was anchored in slots cut in the pipe rim.

NOTE: The holes in the plastic pipe body that let the water enter must be drilled with a drill that cannot wander sideways. A wandering drill in soft material might ruin the job.

Make a special drill with a 2-inch length of 3/4-inch conduit pipe. File teeth in its rim and crimp the other end on a little mandrel, which is turned on a lathe. It should have a protruding pilot pin as shown, which can act as a guide to the drill to prevent wandering. This mandrel can then be clamped into the drill chuck. Naturally, such special tools can serve for similar jobs in the future.

THE VALVE-SEATING DIAPHRAGMS

Over the years I have salvaged things made of copper, and for this job I chose an obsolete photoengraver's copper plate from which to make the valve-seating diaphragm.

Find a similar plate and cut out a disc with a cold chisel. Next, turn from a 3/8-inch thick scrap steel disc a base on which to form the ball-seating diaphragm. The illustration shows how to hammer gradually the edge of the copper disc around the 3/8-inch steel base. Once flanged over that base, the diaphragm will fit perfectly on the three-jaw chuck of the metal-turning lathe. Clamp it on and turn all hammered parts to an accurate fit after drilling a 5/8-inch-diameter hole in its center.

Next, rest the diaphragm on the anvil and place a 3/4-inch-diameter, large ball-bearing ball on the smaller valve hole in the diaphragm. Several gentle hammerblows on the ball will form a spherical seating in the copper, which yields readily to the blows.

It is for an operation like this one that I never pass up the chance to collect the large steel balls from enormous ball bearings when I come across them. Most electric motor repair shops will have some to spare. Being of extreme hardness, they take a heavy hammerblow without denting, but will themselves dent softer material on which they are hammered, thus creating perfectly curved seatings.

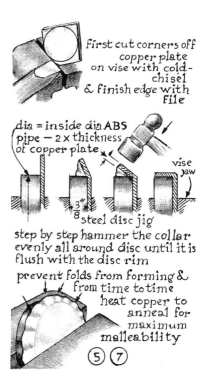

first cut corners off copper plate on vise with cold-chisel & finish edge with file

dia = inside dia ABS pipe — 2 x thickness of copper plate

vise jaw

3/8" steel disc jig

step by step hammer the collar evenly all around disc until it is flush with the disc rim

prevent folds from forming & from time to time heat copper to anneal for maximum malleability

(5) (7)

Making the plunger valve is a little more complicated, but it is somewhat simplified if we keep in mind that none of its parts needs to be machine-accurate. If there is some leakage through backflow of the water it will prove to be insignificant. Up-and-down pumping will open the bottom valve at each stroke and add more water to the column above it, filling the holding tank on top in no time while the bottom valve easily holds it there without leaking.

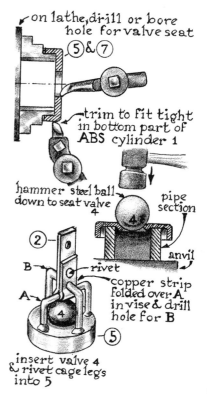

on lathe, drill or bore hole for valve seat

(5) & (7)

trim to fit tight in bottom part of ABS cylinder 1

hammer steel ball down to seat valve 4

pipe section

anvil

(2)

B

A

rivet

copper strip folded over A in vise & drill hole for B

(5)

insert valve 4 & rivet cage legs into 5

Carry out the step-by-step procedure as illustrated and connect the plunger diaphragm to the pump plunger rod with a rivet. Notice from the illustrations how the copper strips are first bent over the pin with light hammering and then clamped in the vise to tighten them together. Next solder the pin and bent-over copper strip. Tin soldering is done best if the contact surfaces of the parts to be soldered are *previously* tinned so that, in assembly, the melting heat causes all tinned surfaces to fuse together easily.

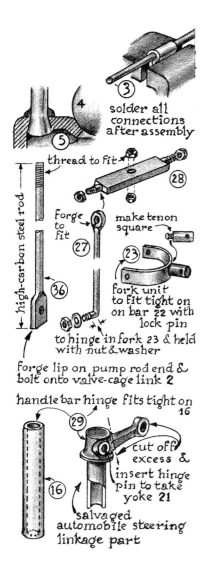

solder all connections after assembly

thread to fit

high-carbon steel rod

Forge to fit

make tenon square

to hinge in fork 23 & held with nut & washer

fork unit to fit tight on on bar 22 with lock pin

forge lip on pump rod end & bolt onto valve-cage link 2

handlebar hinge fits tight on 16

cut off excess & insert hinge pin to take yoke 21

salvaged automobile steering linkage part

THE PLUNGER ROD

Widen by peening the hot end of the high-carbon steel plunger rod in a forging action. Drill a hole in the end to receive the rivet, which fastens it to the plunger valve unit (5).

The top end of the plunger rod is threaded to fit the yoke (28). This yoke has at each end a threaded stub to receive the two linkage rods (27), which in turn allow the forked unit (23) to fit the hooked-over endings of these linkage rods with little nuts and washers. The fork itself is riveted onto a bar (22). This bar is clamped with small bolts between the split yoke parts.

The *yoke* is made with two bars of suitable size and could be angled somewhat to suit the position of the operator in relation to the pumping action.

Hot forge the bar ends into a swage on the anvil to fit the roundness of the fork and handlebars. Depending on where you think the hinging point should be, drill holes in the bars to receive the hinge pins of the hinge body as shown in 29. Now all moving parts can be assembled.

It seems unnecessary to elaborate how the remaining parts of the pump assembly are made and connected, since you will never find yourself in the identical circumstances as I was when gathering material to make those parts. The main thing is to understand the working of the pump, after which inventiveness is in order. You should not hesitate to make the pump as shown; it is very much within your reach to do so, if you use the illustrations simply as guidelines.

This chapter should have made clear that the craftsman with knowledge of machine-shop and blacksmith work never needs to shy away from making everything that he needs.

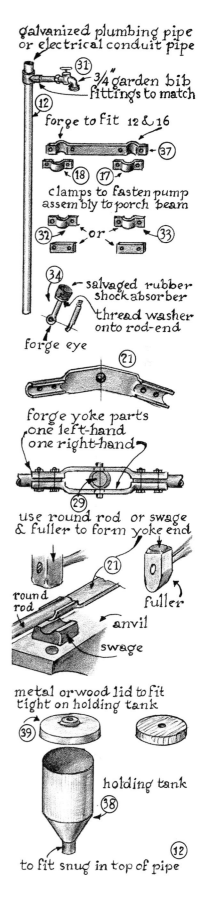

galvanized plumbing pipe
or electrical conduit pipe

31 ¾" garden bib
12 fittings to match

forge to fit 12 & 16

37
18 17

clamps to fasten pump
assembly to porch beam

32 or 33

34 salvaged rubber
shock absorber

thread washer
onto rod-end

forge eye

21

forge yoke parts
one left-hand
one right-hand

29

use round rod or swage
& fuller to form yoke end

21

round
rod

fuller

anvil

swage

metal or wood lid to fit
tight on holding tank

39

holding tank

38

12

to fit snug in top of pipe

6. How to Make a Wood-Turning Lathe and Lathe Tools

a wood-turning lathe made from salvaged materials & inexpensive surplus items

4 bolts & 2 forged straps clamp ball bearings in seat grooves of hardwood headstock to bench

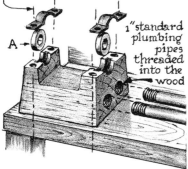

A

1" standard plumbing pipes threaded into the wood

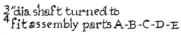

3/4" dia shaft turned to fit assembly parts A-B-C-D-E

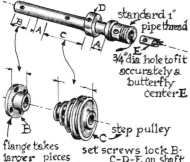

D

standard 1" pipe thread

3/4" dia hole to fit accurately a butterfly center E

flange takes larger pieces outside headstock

set screws lock B-C-D-E on shaft

step pulley

tail stock to have sliding fit on the dual 1¼" lathe bed pipes

Although a simpler wood-turning lathe than the one here presented could be made, readers who already have a well-equipped shop may want to make one that can be used for more than the simplest wood-turning projects.

The main difference between a wood-turning lathe and a metal-turning lathe is in the rigidity of their structures. Turning the larger and heavier pieces will call for a very sturdy lathe.

The four main parts of a lathe are:

1) the *headstock*, which drives the workpiece
2) the *tailstock*, which holds the workpiece aligned and secured between headstock and tailstock
3) the *tool rest*, clasped in an adjustable socket that supports the cutting tool during wood cutting

The tool rest assembly is made so that it can slide over the lathe bed and reach the workpiece over its full length from a fixed position on that bed.

4) the *lathe bed* and its tail end *anchor block*

MAKING THE HEADSTOCK

Use a piece of close-grained hardwood (pear or maple would do) to hold securely the two headstock ball bearings that seat the headstock shaft. The illustration shows how to accomplish it.

Between the bearings the headstock shaft mounts a step pulley and a collar. This pulley is driven by a belt from a counter-step pulley mounted onto an electric motor shaft. This arrangement makes it possible to mount a faceplate outside the lathe headstock shaft extension. Large diameter pieces, which would not fit between headstock and tailstock, can then be turned outside the headstock.

I prefer ball bearings over sleeve bearings, and I use recycled ball bearings since their availability seems unlimited. In the trade, a noisy electrical motor is, as a rule, silenced simply by replacing the noisy ball bearing with a new one, the old one being thrown in the scrap bin. Most of these old bearings are completely adequate for our purpose and are as good as new after they have been greased and/or oiled. Locked up securely in the bearing seatings, they seem to last forever. I have never bought a new ball bearing for any equipment I have made that required bearings. Auto wrecking yards also have ball bearings salvaged from cars damaged beyond repair in highway accidents. We have our choice of the best if we need them, at hardly any cost.

THE HEADSTOCK SPINDLE

Since the threaded end of the headstock is to receive many lathe accessories, I use pipe thread instead of the standard thread in order to utilize much of my salvaged plumbing pipe parts.

You can cut pipe thread on the wood lathe headstock with a standard hand-operated pipe-threading unit. To do this accurately, clamp the headstock spindle in the metal-turning lathe chuck and slip over the free end the thread-cutting die unit. This holds the tailstock sleeve against the die housing to keep all in perfect alignment during cutting of the thread. The tailstock feeds the die during the threading action.

Using the metal lathe headstock in its slowest back-gear drive and steadying the die handle under 90 degrees with axis of rotation, you will be able to cut the thread in alignment to the spindle. If you do not have a metal-turning lathe, clamp the headstock spindle in a vise between brass insets in a perfectly vertical position and cut the thread bit by bit while keeping the path of rotating die handles in an absolutely horizontal path at all times.

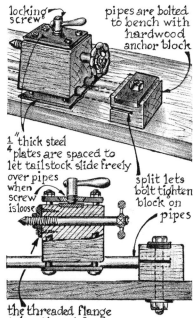

locking screw

pipes are bolted to bench with hardwood anchor block

$\frac{1}{4}$" thick steel plates are spaced to let tailstock slide freely over pipes when screw is loose

split lets bolt tighten block on pipes

the threaded flange takes thrust force on tailstock when work piece is clamped between lathe centers

Once the dies have reached their end position against the spindle shoulder, remove them and turn them upside down so that the smallest diameter thread is now placed over the cone beginning of the headstock thread. Remember that pipe threading dies leave cone threaded pipe endings. Seated and guided by the thread already cut, the same dies will then cut parallel to the axis of rotation leaving a uniform diameter thread.

Remember that cone-threaded pipes are necessary for seating accessories tightly to prevent leaking. The plumbing parts that are to fit the headstock must be rethreaded in a similar way. Do this with the tapering pipe tap by turning the accessory element around and widening its narrow part so that it can be screwed onto the headstock without binding.

CONNECTING THE WOODEN HEADSTOCK BASE TO THE LATHE BED AND TAIL ANCHOR BLOCK

The headstock base and tail anchor block are connected with plumbing pipes, which act as a lathe bed. This bed in turn permits the tool post assembly to slide along its length, to be clamped on at any spot you choose. One end of each pipe is threaded to fit corresponding holes in the headstock, which are threaded with the pipe tap. If you do not have such a tap, you can fashion a makeshift one (for threading wood only) out of the threaded end of scrap plumbing pipe. That end can be fluted with a file or an abrasive cutoff wheel to resemble a professional tap. Made of mild steel, the sharp edges of the thread at the grooved parts will cut through wood very easily.

If you should be tempted to use such a makeshift tap many times it may be useful to harden the thread in the forge fire with case-hardening compound, sold in machinists' and blacksmiths' supply houses. Follow directions on the can.

THE HARDWOOD LATHE BED ANCHOR BLOCK

This also is a block of close-grained hardwood with pipe socket holes to match the ones in the headstock block. Drill the pipe sockets only halfway the length of the block and then split them, as shown,

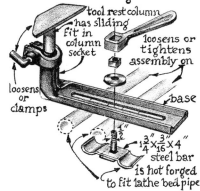

the adjustable tool post for the wood-turning lathe

tool rest column has sliding fit in column socket

loosens or tightens assembly on

loosens or clamps

base

$1\frac{3}{4}$" x $\frac{3}{16}$" x 4" steel bar is hot forged to fit lathe bed pipe

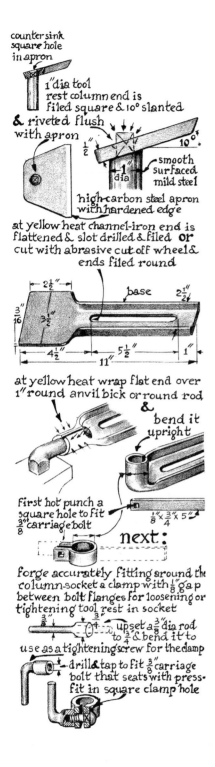

counter sink square hole in apron

1" dia tool rest column end is filed square & 10° slanted & riveted flush with apron

smooth surfaced mild steel

high-carbon steel apron with hardened edge

at yellow heat channel-iron end is flattened & slot drilled & filed **or** cut with abrasive cut off wheel & ends filed round

base

at yellow heat wrap flat end over 1" round anvil bick or round rod **&** bend it upright

first hot punch a square hole to fit ⅜" carriage bolt

next:

forge accurately fitting around the column-socket a clamp with ⅛" gap between bolt flanges for loosening or tightening tool rest in socket

upset a ⅜" dia rod to ¾ & bend it to use as a tightening screw for the clamp

drill & tap to fit ⅜" carriage bolt that seats with press-fit in square clamp hole

so that a bolt placed between pipe holes will clamp the block onto the pipes as well as onto the workbench. Once the lathe bed pipes are thus anchored securely, slide the tailstock center body back and forth over the pipes, which have abrasive paper stuck to them so that the grooves of the tailstock body will become accurately seated.

Oil the wooden seating surface. The oil will penetrate the wood so that all future adjusting of the tailstock over the bed is eased.

MAKING AND FITTING THE TAILSTOCK ONTO THE LATHE BED

First drill the two holes in the tailstock block to fit the dimension of the lathe bed pipe. Bisect these holes with a saw over the full width of the block, separating the two parts. The top part is made to slide along the pipes freely, as shown.

The tailstock center spindle should be pipe-threaded over a considerable length so that maximum adjustments can be made. Fasten a salvaged wheel-shaped water faucet handle to the end of this center to hand turn it. Fasten a threaded flange with pipe thread to the block and install the pipe-threaded center spindle.

If a scrap part is available to turn a little steel flange on a metal-turning lathe, you can use standard thread taps and dies. This makes it possible to use standard bolts and nuts when making the tailstock center screw and spindle.

MAKING AN ADJUSTABLE TOOL POST AND TOOL POST BASE

A short section of channel iron serves as the tool post base. To clamp this base on the lathe bed with 1/2-inch locking bolt, cut a slot so that the tool rest apron itself can be positioned forward, just free from the rotating workpiece.

To make the slot, drill a series of 9/16-inch holes so close together that only a paper-thin thickness of steel is left between each of them. Next place the channel iron between the vise jaws flush with the hole edges and, with a cold chisel, hack in a shearing action through the hole edges. The resulting slot may then be filed clean and smooth.

Or, if you have an abrasive cutoff wheel, you can cut the slot with this abrasive disc. First cut along one side of the slot and next the other, finally freeing the steel remnant at each end with a drill. Clean any irregularities with a rotary file, cold chisel, or grinding points.

To make the tool post socket, heat the slotted channel iron at one end until it is *yellow hot*. Flatten it and, should you lack width to wrap that section around the tool rest collar or a bick of that size, peen it wider.

Next forge the tool rest socket clamp. It should fit around the newly forged column socket as shown. The clamp is to tighten the socket onto the tool apron column so that the desired position of this tool post apron may be locked into place.

One of the aligned holes in the clamp lips is made into a square to fit the square neck of a small carriage bolt. This keeps the bolt from turning when the threaded clamp handle is loosened or tightened. *Or* keep the hole round and use a square-headed bolt that is kept from turning when its square head is held in place by the clamp wall.

CUTTING TOOLS FOR A WOOD-TURNING LATHE

A lengthy vocabulary of names for lathe tools exists, but simpler words for special-purpose tools may better clarify their use. For instance, the first tool shown in the illustration (a) is used to cut most silhouette shapes of a workpiece. When this tool is moved straight and parallel to the lathe bed, the silhouette line will be straight, but if the same tool is moved in a combination of parallel and forward and backward movements, a variation of silhouette shapes can be turned. This is not so with the second and third tools shown (b & c), which have right-angle endings. This type of tool cuts a slot of that width or a wider slot if it is moved to right or left during cutting.

The next tool (d) is simply a narrow cutoff tool to cut off a piece entirely. Often it calls for stopping the lathe, cutting the piece off with a saw just before it drops off, then sanding the cut smooth.

The shallow-curved contouring tool (e) is designed to be held in such a way that only a portion of its width will shave off a thin sliver of the workpiece surface when the refining of a rough surface is called for.

In using all lathe tools you may combine forward motions with side motions, using a pivot point along the tool post apron close to the cutting edge when making circular paths inward or outward to create hollows or spheres.

The tools in the second series of illustrations immediately suggest their uses when we visualize, for instance, what a sharp-pointed tool can do and what round and flat tools cannot do. It is here that we begin to realize that reading long, elaborate explanations is superfluous soon after the beginner finds out for himself the best use of these tools. A little practice with a few basic tools prepares him in a short time to do justice to all the other wood-turning tools designed for special jobs.

Once skilled in working with wood-turning tools, the inventor-craftsman will want to extend his tool collection with a still wider variety with special contours. These can, in one stroke, accomplish a task that would otherwise take several cuts with narrower tools.

To make wider tools, flat leafsprings of cars are ideal. Simply grind them into the needed profiles, taking care during the grinding that the spring steel temper is not lost through overheating. The tools illustrated can in one continued stroke shape a spool, a sphere, a little burin handle.

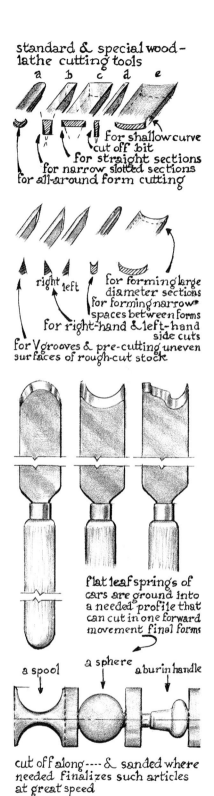

standard & special wood-lathe cutting tools

for shallow curve
cut off bit
for straight sections
for narrow slotted sections
for all-around form cutting

right   left   for forming large diameter sections
for forming narrow spaces between forms
for right-hand & left-hand side cuts
for V grooves & pre-cutting uneven surfaces of rough-cut stock

flat leaf springs of cars are ground into a needed profile that can cut in one forward movement final forms

a spool   a sphere   a burin handle

cut off along ---- & sanded where needed finalizes such articles at great speed

WOOD-TURNING LATHE ACCESSORIES

The tailstock center can have a protruding cone at its work end or have a protruding central pin surrounded by a wide sharp crater rim. The first type of center insert holds the workpiece by the tip of the cone only. In the other, the lead pin penetrates the wood entirely until the polished crater's cutting edge becomes imbedded in the wood, thus holding the workpiece more securely than would the single point at the cone end.

The total surface of the crater rim that is imbedded into the wood should be greased somewhat to reduce friction during turning of the workpiece. The odor of scorched wood will soon tell you that the tailstock needs attention. If the wood should scorch around the crater cup, a little candle wax rubbed over the groove created by the crater edge often is sufficient to stop the scorching.

Tailstock Centers

If you have a metal-turning lathe you can make a variety of tailstock centers that have welcome features.

One type is the *open cup center*. It will hold a piece of wood that may not be entirely round. The workpiece will seek its own center and form its own seating in such a cup. Under friction an uneven wood ending would wear somewhat under compression into an even fit. After a little lubrication, cutting can start right away.

This system bypasses the need for an exact centering of the workpiece with a predrilled hole. When you use a deep cup center, the workpiece cannot be pushed out of its seating during the full run of the turning operation. The cup leaves no central hole, but some end trimming may be required afterward.

The *ball bearing center* is a very useful design you can make on the metal-turning lathe. First forge onto the stock end a wide head, which can be turned into an exact seating socket to hold a ball bearing very tightly. Next, turn a small center insert with a little protruding seating pin that fits snugly in the ball bearing hole. This system eliminates all tail center friction during wood cutting. I find myself using this type of center more than any other.

Another design has a socket with a locking screw, as illustrated. It can take a small solid cone insert or a little crater center or a small wide cup center with a leading pin. If the pin is left out entirely the wide cup can take many irregular workpieces in a self-centering action.

Other types of center arrangements are shown also; they are all variations of the same principle and serve to hold the workpiece in alignment with the headstock drive during the cutting action.

wood turning lathe head stock & tail stock-center designs

if head & tailstock have Morse taper sockets, then all matching taper centers are interchangeable

standard cone-center & cup center snug fit

wood stock ends that fit roughly in wide cup centers become self-centered

ball bearing press-fit

tailstock assembly lets ball bearing rotate the center insert with minimum stock friction

set screw locks

all center inserts to have same shank size

snug sliding fit on taper end shoulder

sockets to fit snug over shoulder

ball bearing is press-fit into socket

interchangeable inserts

if headstock socket has Morse taper, then center inserts don't need set screw locking

The Headstock Center

This must hold the workpiece firmly anchored to the headstock spindle. If the headstock spindle has no Morse taper socket, then a cylindrical socket must seat a cylindrical-centered shank as exactly as possible and be held in position by a set screw.

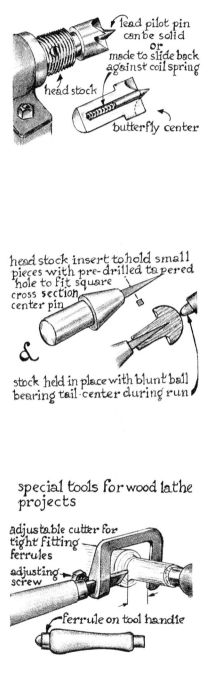

lead pilot pin can be solid
or
made to slide back against coil spring

head stock

butterfly center

The butterfly, or four-wing, design of the center and its leading pin will leave the wood workpiece marked with a small central hole and four deep indentations, because the wing teeth must be pressed deep enough into the wood to drive the workpiece. You can improve this design with a sliding pilot pin that retracts on a coiled spring so that the pin slides back after its point has been placed on a previously marked center of the workpiece. When the workpiece is pressed onto the butterfly center, the pilot pin will be completely depressed, leaving hardly any mark in the wood.

This refinement may seem to be gilding the lily, since the little markings do no harm to a tool's functioning, and, after some hammering, the compacted wood closes up the remnants of such shallow markings. All the same, any handle, and a tool handle especially, looks better without markings of that sort.

head stock insert to hold small pieces with pre-drilled tapered hole to fit square cross section center pin

&

stock held in place with blunt ball bearing tail-center during run

Inventiveness leads to the making of specialized tools. Not everyone cares to spend the time to make them if they are not used often. If, however, I intend to make large quantities of duplicate workpieces, I can justify designing a special tool that will improve the appearance of the pieces over and above their usefulness.

When making many small artifacts, such as small burin handles, for instance, one can design a jig as described in Chapter 16. Another special tool can be designed to hold a small handle while its marked ends are cleaned up. A long, square cross section pin holds the workpiece while a blunt ball bearing tail center keeps it from sliding off the pin during the run.

Adjustable Cutters

I have found it useful to reinforce heavy-duty tool handles with steel ferrules to prevent the wood from splitting. To get the right ferrule-seating dimension, you can make a cutter gauge. Its first cut establishes the needed dimension. Other tools can follow up the first cut to the finished ferrule seating. In this way it is not necessary to stop and start the lathe in order to measure sizes with calipers. The gauge assures the correct diameter for a press fit of ferrule on wood under great force. Since the gauge can be adjusted to whatever size you need, the saving of time and effort when many handles are to be made will justify making this tool.

special tools for wood lathe projects

adjustable cutter for tight fitting ferrules

adjusting screw

ferrule on tool handle

Using a Cutter Gauge

First cut each end of the workpiece stock freehand into a small cone shape. This makes it possible to slip the cutter gauge over the cone. The clearance between the cutter itself and the wood is closed in a self-adjusting action during a first cut. After this, any standard cutting tool can follow up and finish the rest.

You may be tempted to use that cutter gauge to cut the entire section you need for the ferrule seating. If so, you will have to redesign the cutter edges in order to facilitate this operation. It will be a little difficult to prevent certain uncontrolled forward movements of the tool should a false move make it "grab" the wood, thus immediately cutting the wood diameter smaller than you intended. Or, it may leave a deep local groove that reduces the hold of the ferrule seating and the handle's strength where it is most needed. After some exploration, you may decide to leave well enough alone and simply use this adjustable cutter as a dimension indicator for a first cut, to be followed up with freehand cutting.

Tailored Tool Rests

Besides straight tool rest aprons of various lengths, you may need an extra long one. For such a one it is best to make supporting columns, one at each end, fitting in corresponding tool sockets. If such an extra long tool rest only has one central post, support its ends with a wedge arrangement between their ends and the lathe bed. This will eliminate possible downward vibrations of the tool rest during the turning of the wood. Downward vibrations in a "springy" apron can wreak havoc with the workpiece since any sudden interference with a steady cut makes the tool end grab the wood, leaving a deep groove or torn wood surface.

A tailored tool rest apron is called for if you plan to turn deep, hollow parts, such as a wooden bowl. The illustrations are self-explanatory and do not need a lengthy text. What may require further description is the manner of attaching a workpiece (such as a wooden bowl) to a faceplate, which can be done without wood screws by *gluing* the piece directly to the faceplate.

The best way to do this is to first screw onto the faceplate a piece of plywood, which is then turned to the needed dimension. On the surface of this plywood, glue, with a strong adhesive, a piece of cardboard, to which in turn the workpiece is glued. The glue may be a contact cement or any other type of strong adhesive. The holding force in this arrangement is very reliable if application is done correctly. When the turning is finished, detach the piece by splitting the cardboard in two with a broad, thin chisel. The separation comes quite easily, leaving the base of the workpiece unmarked by screw seatings.

Plumbing Parts as Lathe Accessories

The most used is the *floor flange*. Because the threaded part has been tapered so that it will clamp itself on a plumbing pipe ending, the narrow part of the floor flange thread must be widened until it can easily be screwed on the headstock without binding. A cylindrical threading tap can be used to accomplish the widening. Or, use the standard taper tap to open the narrow end of the flange from the other side until the flange is free of binding on the headstock.

If you decide to make such a tap, use an adjustable standard pipe-threading die and cut the thread on a bar of annealed high-carbon steel. Grind the tap flutings with an abrasive cutoff wheel and finally harden the tap by quenching in oil at *cherry red* heat glow, which gives it the hardness of a cold chisel edge.

Final fitting of the floor flange on the headstock calls for refining the contact area between the flange hub and the headstock shoulder face. If these two seat exactly after tightening, the flange "facing" can be turned in position for accuracy with a hand-held *carbon-tipped* lathe tool. Hold this tool firmly on the steady rest, which has been

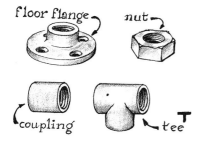

wood bowl

tool is moved along apron

tool rest apron

gap is to be closed from time to time during work cut when finished

workbench

tool rest made for bowl-turning is contoured to reduce the gap between wood & apron edge

floor flange

nut

coupling

tee

placed with its apron edge as close as possible to, but free from the flange rotation. Holding down the tool firmly so it has the least possible chance of wandering, cut the metal in a scraping or shaving action. After all inaccurate parts have been cut away, the flange is ready to receive, with four wood screws, a plywood facing, as described before.

Any workpiece used *without* that plywood disc can be screwed directly onto the floor flange.

Abrasive Discs and Side Grinders

Making several such floor flange attachments means you can fasten to them plywood discs of various sizes to which can be attached abrasive papers for the many wood surface sanding jobs you may have to do. A disc cut from salvaged offset printing rubber blankets can be glued on first to soften the abrasive action when finally abrasive sheets are glued onto the rubber-sided discs.

The plywood disc, after it has been accurately faced, may have glued to it an abrasive cutoff disc to make a side-grinder. Such grinders, as described before, can grind accurate flat surfaces on metal workpieces.

Wood-Turning Lathe Headstocks as Grinding Arbors

Grinding wheels with large lead bores sometimes fit directly on headstocks. It so happens that a thread on a 3/4-inch plumbing pipe has an outside dimension of 1 inch, which coincides with many large grinding wheel bores.

As a rule, such large surplus or salvaged but worn wheels can be purchased at flea markets at little cost. The advantage becomes apparent if you can slip them onto the headstock ends without having to make adapters. The wheel's lead hole walls cannot harm the thread on the headstock. Therefore, if the wheel is locked up between two washers and a plumbing pipe nut, you have achieved an uncomplicated and sturdy arrangement.

In addition, the step pulley allows you to change the wheel's rpm to the one you feel is the most effective and safe. Adjust the regular tool rest so that no gap remains between it and the wheel after the wheel has been dressed to accuracy.

standard plumbing pipe fittings having same thread size of lathe head-stock, can serve to fasten most variety of stock & accessories

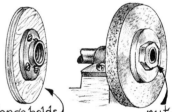

flange holds plywood disc on which are glued abrasive sheets

nut holds grinding wheels

WARNING: Any grinding with a lathe requires that the lathe be protected from *abrasive residues* that fly off the wheel during work and may creep between critical bearing surfaces or enter parts that slide together. Place paper or drop-cloth covers over endangered surfaces during grinding. After the job is done, clean carefully to remove the last trace of abrasive powders. If you have an air compressor, a forced air blast removes the abrasive dust best.

7. Tempering High-Carbon Steel

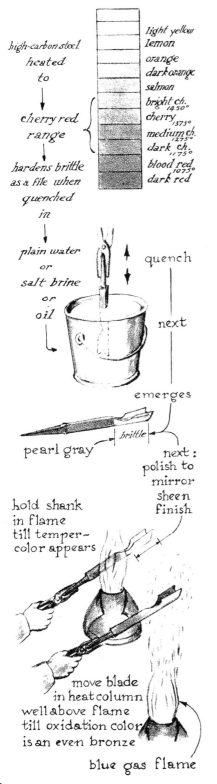

high-carbon steel
heated
to
↓
cherry red
range
↓
hardens brittle
as a file when
quenched
in
↓
plain water
or
salt brine
or
oil
↓

light yellow
lemon
orange
dark orange
salmon
bright ch. 1450°
cherry 1375°
medium ch. 1275°
dark ch. 1175°
blood red 1075°
dark red

quench

next

emerges

pearl gray | brittle

next:
polish to
mirror
sheen
finish

hold shank
in flame
till temper-
color appears

move blade
in heat column
well above flame
till oxidation color
is an even bronze

blue gas flame

In shop practice, it is preferable to quench hot high-carbon steel first to *file hardness*, which is *brittle hardness*.

To make high-carbon steel brittle hard, it must have a visible heat glow of *light cherry red* to *dark yellow* at the moment of quench. After this quench it is reheated over a blue flame to subtract excess hardness until it reaches the hardness of your choice. This process is called *tempering*.

A faster method, but one with greater risk of misjudgment, involves quenching hot steel directly to its final hardness. This is called *hardening* and does not require tempering afterward.

The *quenching liquid*, as a rule, is water, but may be brine, oil, fat, or other suitable coolant. In the blacksmith shop the coolants all assume room temperature. At moment of quench, the shock impact between the heat of the hot tool and the room temperature liquid is the same regardless of the liquid used. After the moment of impact, however, the submerged steel cools at different rates in different liquids, depending on the boiling point of each; water boils at 100°C. (212°F.), oils and fats at 300°C. (572°F.).

After the quench the brittle part is made shiny by grinding and polishing. That part is next reheated over a blue flame (the kitchen stove gas flame or the flame of a blow torch will do). At first the shiny part of the tool is kept out of the flame so that the softer part of the tool is heated first, allowing the heat to travel by conduction to the shiny part. In due time *oxidation colors* will appear on the shiny steel surface, creating a color spectrum that travels, through conduction, outward to the tool's cutting edge as the heat is continually increased.

The first color to appear in this spectrum will be *faint straw*, followed by *dark straw*; *bronze*; *peacock*; *purple*; *full blue*; *light blue*, and finally *faint blue resembling blue gray*. The drawing of these colors can be arrested at any time you choose by quenching in water.

Faint straw indicates the correct hardness for wood-engraving burins, razors, scribes, and all tools that are not strained much, but are given the hardest edges that stay sharp longest.

Straw is the hardness for hatchets, axes, and comparable tools.

Dark straw is good for cold chisels, stone carving tools, punches, dies, and thick-bladed woodcutting tools.

Bronze is best for sturdy-bladed woodcutting tools that are used with hammers on medium and hard woods.

Peacock, which is a blend of bronze and purple, is best for most thin-bladed wood-carving gouges.

Purple matches the hardness for springs, spatulas, table knives.

Full blue is for gun barrels, machine parts such as bearing housings, steel brackets.

Light blue is too soft for cutting tools but may serve for handles, levers, parts that do not require springiness.

Faint blue resembling gray, the last color in the spectrum, means that the high-carbon steel has been annealed to its softest and can be turned on the lathe or drilled, milled or filed, as one can do with mild steel.

In hardening high-carbon steel files and rasps, no colors need to be drawn and brittle quenching only is required. High-carbon steel emerges from the quenching bath with a pearl gray hue. Most temperable steels found in the scrap pile can be tempered in this way.

The process of tempering high-carbon steel is in time less complicated as it becomes understood clearly. The variables involved give the smith-toolmaker a welcome chance to be inventive in choosing the combination of steps he must follow for best results.

For further information, the reader can find extended descriptions on the art of tempering in my two previous books, *The Making of Tools* and *The Modern Blacksmith*, published by Van Nostrand Reinhold.

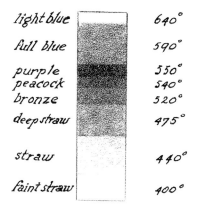

light blue	640°
full blue	590°
purple	550°
peacock	540°
bronze	520°
deep straw	475°
straw	440°
faint straw	400°

oxidation color spectrum on all steel surfaces when heated gradually

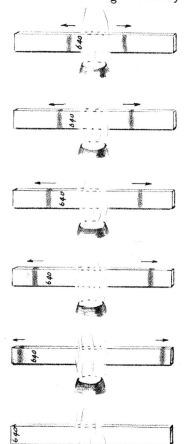

oxidation colors during heat-treating of high-carbon steel

8. Making Carbon-Tipped Tools for Wood- and Metal-Turning Lathes

steel may be turned on a wood-turning lathe if tools are carbon tipped ⟶

use ⟶
tips silver soldered onto mild steel bars that are hand held
use same tips, silver soldered on high-carbon steel bar, if used in tool post of metal-turning lathe

steel turned in wood lathe

at low 800-1000 rpm, steel bar held by chuck and tail center in a wood lathe can be cut by hand-held carbon tip tools

a face plate & dog are used if no chuck is available

Carbon-tipped steel cutting tools that are sold today to take the place of the high-carbon steel ones have two advantages: (1) their hardness will not diminish when the tool heats up and (2) their hardness is so great that they can cut even hardened high-carbon steel. But the disadvantages are that any undue shock on a carbon tip will, as a rule, break it. Also, if the sharp edge gets lodged during a cutting action it is almost impossible to extract the tool without breaking its edge.

Tool bars for metal-turning should be made of high-carbon steel measuring approximately 3/8 inch by 3/4 to 1 inch. A bar is clamped into the tool post of a fairly heavy-duty metal-turning lathe and a carbon tip can then be soldered onto it. Because of the great strains that often occur during metal turning, *silver solder* is used instead of tin solder to bond the tips to the bars.

Sections of mild or high-carbon steel bars can be made into wood-turning tools with tangs at one end to take long wooden handles. Or, they can be kept short without tangs, to be clamped in tool posts for metal-turning.

Wood-turning seldom requires carbon-tipped lathe tools. Occasionally, however, you will have to trim a metal part in a wood-turning project and will need a carbon-tipped tool to do it. This happens, for example, when a finished tool handle with metal ferrules on each end needs some trimming on the lathe. Used as a wood-turning tool, the carbon tip actually scrapes or shaves the metal, since the depth of the cut is always very slight.

If you do not have a metal-turning lathe it is possible in an emergency to cut steel on a wood-turning lathe. There must, however, be a way to fasten the steel workpiece in the wood lathe headstock and reduce the rpm to about 500.

Adjust the tool post height so that the cutting edge level of the carbon tip will be at the center level of the workpiece. Keep the gap between the tool post apron and the workpiece as small as possible. In action the tool must be held down extra firmly to prevent it from being caught between the workpiece and the tool post apron. Steel bars can be reduced in this way—little by little to the wanted sizes—with hand-held carbon-tipped tools. This method was practiced extensively in the nineteenth century, when hardened high-carbon steel cutting edges were used to cut metal. A very low rpm of the lathe headstock was maintained to keep the tool edge from heating up.

SOLDERING METALS TOGETHER

Soldering metals resembles somewhat the technique of welding. In both instances it is important that the oxygen in the air not reach the melt. This can be accomplished by surrounding the melting area with a substance that keeps the oxygen out but at the same time does not interfere with the fusing of the solder on the surfaces to be bonded together.

In silver soldering a borax flux keeps the oxygen away from the metals. Zinc-saturated muriatic acid applied to the metal surfaces degreases all the pores, which will then, as a rule, accept the bonding metal at the point of its melt; the zinc element acts as a catalyst.

In silver soldering a borox flux keeps the oxygen away from the surface as well as from the melted solder. At the moment of melt the flux will be pushed aside by the solder flow. At the point of bonding it seems as though the two metal surfaces were drawn together automatically.

Failures usually can be traced to oxygen interference, which introduces oxidation scales between the surfaces. After a failure, you must scrape surfaces completely clean before attempting soldering again.

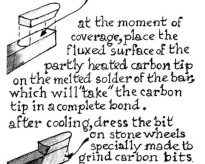

brush standard silver solder flux over clean & accurate surface of bar & heat it in forge fire cherry red as seen in semi dark room

next: silver solder wire end is held on fluxed surface and its "melt" evenly distributed over the whole surface

at the moment of coverage, place the fluxed surface of the partly heated carbon tip on the melted solder of the bar, which will "take" the carbon tip in a complete bond.

after cooling, dress the bit on stone wheels specially made to grind carbon bits.

It is often puzzling to the beginner why the best soldering job is the one for which only a minimum of solder is used. Excessive solder between two unmatched surfaces weakens the joint markedly.

Although brazing and welding pieces of steel together are not covered in this book, the same principles apply.

METAL-TURNING WITH CARBON-TIPPED TOOLS, HIGH-SPEED TOOLS, AND HIGH-CARBON TOOLS

In spite of the advantages that carbon-tipped tools and high-speed steel cutting tips have, they do not replace entirely correctly hardened high-carbon steel cutting tools in the home workshop.

If it proves too difficult to silver-solder carbon tips to bar stock, or if you do not have high-speed cutting tips, you can always fall back on the much easier way of making metal-turning cutting tools from good quality high-carbon steel. In my experience it is quite sufficient to have high-carbon steel tools without special alloys. They serve excellently if you don't speed the cutting. (Excessive speed overheats and ruins the temper of the tool.) It is also important to remember that the workpiece must be *softer* than the cutting tool.

The desirable thing is to purchase high-speed steel lathe cutting tips, if possible. These tips, though a little less hard than well-hardened high-carbon tips, or well-hardened high-carbon steel edges, have the advantage that they will not be dulled appreciably by excessive heat created during the cutting of metal at high speed.

Remember, however, that the well-tempered edge of a high-carbon steel cutting bit will, as a rule, fill most of your needs. It is encouraging to know you can do without all of the fancy modern alloy steels, so indispensible to a sophisticated modern industry, as long as you are *not in a hurry, the cutting speed of the lathe is low*, and you have *easy access to high-carbon steel.* You will find to your pleasure that in all respects the scrap pile and metal-turning in a home shop go hand in hand.

One item sometimes found in the scrap pile is like a gem. It is the *magnet.* The early automobiles had V-shaped magnets in their generators. Old Fords also used to have them. These have proven to be excellent stock from which to make tools.

Magnets will retain their magnetism at their best if the steel they are made from has the highest possible carbon content and has been made as hard as possible. Be careful in quenching a magnet, however, since there is a danger that the steel could crack at the moment it is quenched in cold or freezing liquids. Several magnets that I tried to forge into tools turned out to be worthless since they were full of cracks. But I did find other perfect ones and was able to make the very best lathe cutting tools out of them. Take the chance if this type of magnet should come your way; if they are without cracks, the time you spend making lathe cutting tools from them will not be wasted.

9. How to Drill Square Holes

Admittedly this knowledge is of limited use. There are several ways to make square holes without drilling them and they are preferred by industry. Drilling a square hole actually combines *drilling* with *milling*, during which the tool is guided by a brittle-hard, square-holed jig attached to the workpiece.

In woodworking, square holes are made with drills that rotate within a square, sharp-ended housing that acts as a chisel in the downward thrust. This instrument is a combination drill and broach. In metalwork, a broach is the instrument that shears the steel in a downward thrust. The four corners around a predrilled hole are cut this way without the use of the drill.

DESIGN PRINCIPLE OF THE CUTTER

As the illustrations show, the sides of the equilateral triangle placed in the square have the same length as the sides of the square and thus can move within the square without binding. If that triangle is modified into a configuration with curved, instead of straight, sides, it will then move within the limits of the square with three of its sides and one of its points always touching and sliding along the square's sides. The points of this configuration, however, meeting at an angle a little larger than 90 degrees, cannot fit into the square jig's 90-degree corners and must bypass them somewhat. It therefore describes a square with slightly rounded corners.

If the drill is made with sharp corners, straight sides, and a flat cutting-face, it will not act like a regular drill with the cone-shaped profile of its self-centering cutting edges. A cone-shaped cutting profile would cause the drill to seek its center of rotation automatically. With the cutting edges in a flat plane, however, the drill is allowed to wander in whatever direction the cutting forces dictate. It is here that the brittle-hard square jig, when fastened to the workpiece, is used to confine the drill's motions to a wobbling one, forcing it to slide along the square's sides as dictated by the jig, at the same time as it cuts away the steel below it.

It is best to make the drill shank as long as possible in order to cut the sides of the hole as parallel as possible to the axis of rotation. Note that the wobbling action of the milling end is made possible by the springiness of the long drill shank.

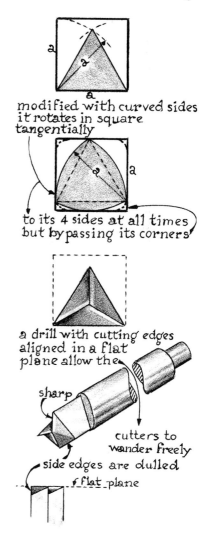

an equilateral triangle in a square as shown can rotate in it without binding

modified with curved sides it rotates in square tangentially

to its 4 sides at all times but bypassing its corners

a drill with cutting edges aligned in a flat plane allow the

sharp

cutters to wander freely

side edges are dulled

flat plane

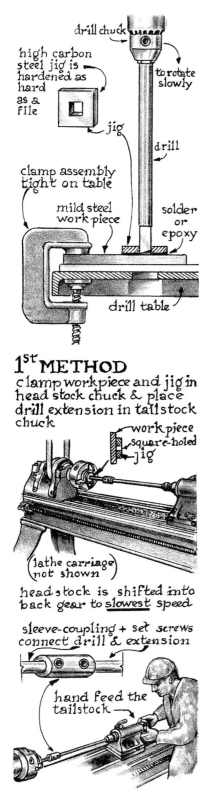

drill chuck

high carbon
steel jig is
hardened as
hard
as a
file

to rotate
slowly

jig

drill

clamp assembly
tight on table

mild steel
work piece

solder
or
epoxy

drill table

1ˢᵗ METHOD
clamp workpiece and jig in
head stock chuck & place
drill extension in tailstock
chuck

work piece
square-holed
jig

(lathe carriage)
not shown

head stock is shifted into
back gear to slowest speed

sleeve-coupling + set screws
connect drill & extension

hand feed the
tailstock

The workpiece and jig can be clamped together on the table of the drill press. An alternate arrangement, clamping workpiece and jig in the chuck of a metal-turning lathe that has a long bed, renders the cone effect of the hole negligible. The rod extension of the shank with a sleeve coupling gives us a maximum shank length. Thus the tailstock is placed at a great distance from the rotating headstock while the drill is fed by the tailstock.

Another method uses a short stubby drill. The combined jig and workpiece are placed on a roller swivel-bearing or on a stack of well-lubricated flat, smooth discs that act as a swivel bearing.

It is amusing to demonstrate the drilling of square holes to unbelievers who are not acquainted with this procedure. I first saw it done on my last day in school in 1923 in Holland, where I was trained to be a marine engineer. The teacher in the machine shop demonstrated how to drill a square hole, thus enlivening the occasion of graduation. But on a later occasion, when I served in the Netherlands East Indies conscript army as a private in the ordnance plant, I was challenged to prove my claim that I could drill square holes. I was given the opportunity to do so, and after witnessing this feat my superiors saw fit to qualify me, then and there, as sergeant instead of private.

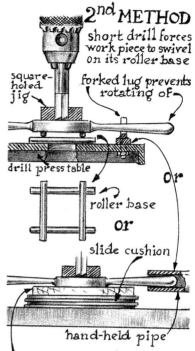

2nd METHOD
short drill forces work piece to swivel on its roller base

square-holed jig

forked lug prevents rotating of

drill press table

or

roller base

or

slide cushion

hand-held pipe

wood base placed on a few oiled smooth sheet metal discs allows free swivel movements of work piece

10. Making Hand-Held Punches

circle-pattern punches made from high-carbon steel rods & seamless tubular steel

made of various sizes

Spread while hot into cone with drifts

sharpen edge if it must cut **or** keep it dull if it is to form a low relief only

hardwood handle to fit cone socket

rubber blanket on

wood block

relief designs made with sets of circle-pattern punches

&

sets of graded cup-end rod punches to cut holes **or** raise button shapes if struck short of cutting the sheet

sets of graded ball-ends punches that form depressions

upset, drill & grind

temper straw after brittle quench in oil

rubber blanket

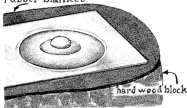

hard wood block

First use ball-end punches from below sheet before cutting a disc free to prevent buckling of edges

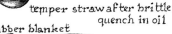

The punches are used to cut or indent thin sheets of metal or other sheet material into various shapes and designs. Simple patterns can be cut using steel tubes with sharpened ends. If the tubes are made from high-carbon steel, they will stand up better than those made from mild steel, the edges of which are too soft. Mild steel tubes have to be case-hardened at the cutting edge, which will last well when not abused.

Once in a while one finds on the scrap pile a seamless high-carbon steel tube. Seam-welded mild steel tubes, used in the plumbing trade and for electrical conduit tubes, are more readily available.

The illustrations show how a seamless tube, heated in the forge fire, can be flared out with a cutting edge at one end and a handle socket at the other. Be sure to harden all punch ends to the hardness of a cold chisel.

To use a punch designed as shown, prepare a wood stump with a smooth surface. Glue onto it a piece of rubber blanket salvaged from an offset printing shop. As a base upon which to punch out designs from sheet metal and other thin material, it resists being cut or marred. One can generally purchase for very little money, also from such a printing shop, discarded aluminum sheets.

Placed on the stump, the soft metal can be cut with one fairly hard blow of the hammer on the punch, making a clean hole through the metal. Or, a lighter blow will leave an uncut indentation with a low relief effect. The design surface can be raised still more, if desired, with a punch ending in a partial sphere.

These two types of punches are rather easy to make, and it is a good idea to make several sizes in order to extend the design possibilities. The large range of punch designs shown provides the opportunity for inventing whatever shapes you may need.

USING SPRING STEEL FOR MAKING PUNCHES

Leaf springs and coil springs from cars are ideal for making punches. Engine push rods, many linkage rods, and most car parts—because they are inherently resilient—are, as a rule, made from temperable steel. This makes it possible to harden the cutting edge of tools made from them.

Special Punches for Decorative Designs

For a 2-inch wide punch in the shape of a heart, there is an advantage in making the pattern in two halves—one left- and one right-hand punch, each the opposite of the other. Combined they make a heart profile; individually they can be used to make many other designs.

Take a 6- to 8-inch long section of a leaf spring of a car. Heat it on one end and peen it out to about 4 inches wide. Heat the other end and upset it into a head. Sharpen the wide, flat end and grind it with an outside bevel so that the head position, aligned with the center of gravity of the cutting pattern, will spread the force of the hammer-blow evenly over the full cutting edge.

Make the reverse punch with a template cut by the first punch. When this template is turned over it becomes its opposite.

Another punch design can be forged from a similar blank. Heat the blade and shape it over rod ends that act as bicks. The edge of the punch will form a three-quarter circle. In the same way, other punch endings can be shaped with curve designs hammered out on props made especially for them.

A series of punches using similar blanks make variations of three-quarter, half, and quarter moons. The punches described so far are especially suited for making interconnected designs without cutting them away from the sheet. Closed circular punches that are made to cut all the way through can be held slanted and used to cut partially through to form half circles.

Punches can be shaped to cut out squares, parallelograms, rosettes, stars—whatever figures the design calls for.

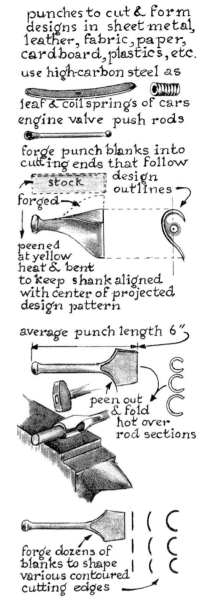

punches to cut & form designs in sheet metal, leather, fabric, paper, cardboard, plastics, etc. use high-carbon steel as

leaf & coil springs of cars engine valve push rods

forge punch blanks into cutting ends that follow design outlines

stock

forged

peened at yellow heat & bent to keep shank aligned with center of projected design pattern

average punch length 6"

peen out & fold hot over rod sections

forge dozens of blanks to shape various contoured cutting edges

if mild steel tubes
are used

cutting edges
are to be casehardened

up set rod ends are turned on the
lathe & tempered to straw
hardness both ends

high-carbon tube ends are
formed at yellow heat over
pre-shaped rod ends

file, grind
saw, chisel,
chase a tapered rod end

You may be tempted to use plumbing pipes to make such punches with case-hardened edges. Some of them, if not large enough, can be made larger by upsetting or spreading the end. For heavy work, however, use only high-carbon steel pipe.

WARNING: The galvanized surfaces of plumbing pipes around the working ends of tools must be ground off. Heating the punch end with the zinc coating left on will ruin the quality of the steel and make case hardening ineffective. I have successfully made cutting punches after grinding away the zinc coating, then beveling the edges to razor sharpness before case hardening them.

Remember that the cutting edges of all mild steel tools that have been case hardened should never be sharpened on *both* sides since the case-hardening compound does not penetrate very deeply. Sharpening both sides will leave a soft core edge, whereas sharpening one side only will leave the other sharp edge hard.

The working ends of all high-carbon steel tools should be annealed before they are filed into the endless variety of design contours, as the examples show.

Even if your punches seem strong and well-tempered, do not use them on a steel that may be too hard.

Using Car Axle Ends as Stock

Chapter 26 in this book explains how to free a car axle from its flange and ball bearing. You will, as a rule, have between two and three inches diameter of solid material from its end to work with.

Cut a length that can be conveniently hand held as a punch. Anneal it in the fire and turn the end into a *flat facing* on the lathe. Proceed as shown in the illustration or, instead of gluing the paper design onto the facing, blacken it with ink or a mixture of lampblack and grease. Wipe it off, leaving a little black residue.

Next, draw the design on this black facing using a pair of dividers in measured-off center-punch marks. Whichever method of design transfer you use, the correct placing of center-punch marks will enable you to place the drill depressions evenly.

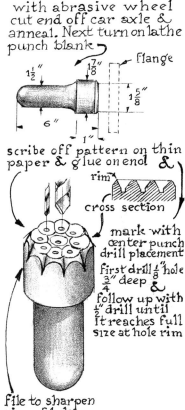

with abrasive wheel
cut end off car axle &
anneal. Next turn on lathe
punch blank

Flange

scribe off pattern on thin
paper & glue on end &
rim

cross section

mark with
center punch
drill placement

first drill ⅛" hole
¾" deep &

follow up with
½" drill until
it reaches full
size at hole rim

file to sharpen
rims of holes

Place the shank of the punch in the vise and file away all superfluous material along the design outline until the bevel edge is *almost* as sharp as you finally want it. The very final sharpness can be reached easily with the aid of a small, rubber-backed abrasive disc rotating at high speed in a fixed grinding arbor. You can then grind off the resulting fine burr or feather edge on a tripoli-impregnated cotton buffer. This gives the punch the cutting edge it needs to easily cut out a small rosette with one hard hammerblow. Or, using a lesser blow, you can simply indent a rosette design, and then make it more pronounced by turning it over and, using a spherical tool, hammering it repoussé style to accent the raised relief.

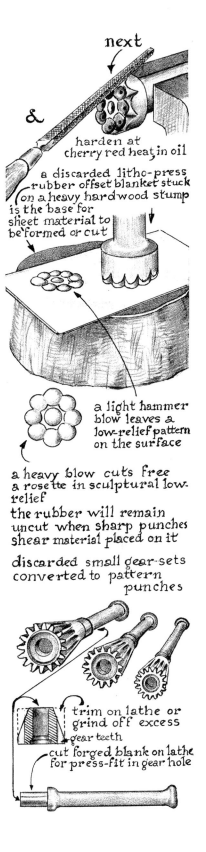

next

&

harden at cherry red heat, in oil

a discarded litho-press rubber offset blanket stuck on a heavy hardwood stump is the base for sheet material to be formed or cut

a light hammer blow leaves a low-relief pattern on the surface

a heavy blow cuts free a rosette in sculptural low-relief

the rubber will remain uncut when sharp punches shear material placed on it

discarded small gear-sets converted to pattern punches

trim on lathe or grind off excess gear teeth

cut forged blank on lathe for press-fit in gear hole

Punches Made from Odds and Ends of Scrap

The little pinion gears fastened to the ends of rods are often found at scrap steel yards, and can be used to make punches. Many odd machine parts from dismantled equipment can also be converted into punches to leave indentations, as shown.

A somewhat more elaborate combination, not too difficult to make, uses a cluster of engine push rods with cup-shaped endings. Used singly, these endings can serve as individual punches, but clustered they can punch out rosette designs. In many combinations these punches can make very decorative patterns, which can be accentuated by relief techniques.

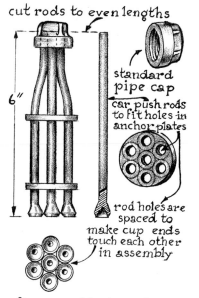

cut rods to even lengths

6"

standard pipe cap

car push rods to fit holes in anchor plates

rod holes are spaced to make cup ends touch each other in assembly

after assembly heat the 7 rod ends yellow hot & force bundled rod ends tightly in pipe-cap

next: reheat pipe cap end & forge it to fill all remaining clearance between cap & rods

unsharpened cup rims, when punched on soft sheet metal, will leave sculptural relief patterns, provided

the sheet rests on a rubber blanket glued to the smooth flat top of a heavy hardwood stump

More complicated machine parts may take a little more time to fabricate, but they are well within reach of the craftsman who has come this far in his ability to make just about every tool he needs from waste material. The illustrations here are self-explanatory.

How to Make the Star Punch

Punch the cold, hard male die into the soft *yellow-hot* seating, which yields like clay. During hammering the seating begins to cool, but at the same time it begins to heat up the cold male die. Do not continue hammering the hot seating after it has cooled off too much.

Remove the die and cool it in the quenching liquid for a few seconds. This in turn allows the seating (should there be enough reserve heat) to reheat the cooled off portion to forgeable heat. Carefully reseat the male die and deliver once more a few heavy blows before the seat again has become too cold for continued hammering.

Resist the temptation to keep on hammering; reheat the seating part whenever necessary. Cool off the male die before the next round of shaping the blank.

That same die can shape various sizes of star punches. Simply increase the depth of penetration into the female head, leaving progressively larger or smaller impressions as you wish. Having a choice of sizes of star punches makes it possible to create the design shown in the illustration. They can be used to *imprint* a low-relief decorative design on the sheet or to *cut out* a medallion-type rosette form.

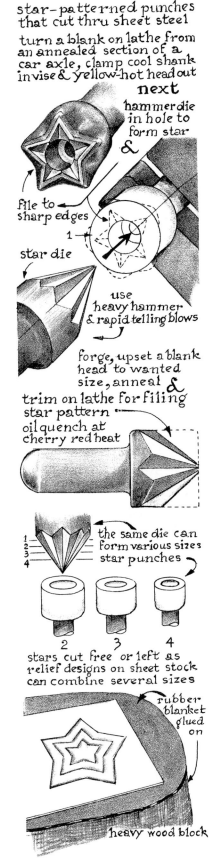

star-patterned punches that cut thru sheet steel

turn a blank on lathe from an annealed section of a car axle, clamp cool shank in vise & yellow-hot head out

next

hammer die in hole to form star &

File to sharp edges

1

star die

use heavy hammer & rapid telling blows

forge, upset a blank head to wanted size, anneal & trim on lathe for filing star pattern oil quench at cherry red heat

1
2
3
4

the same die can form various sizes star punches

2   3   4

stars cut free or left as relief designs on sheet stock can combine several sizes

rubber blanket glued on

heavy wood block

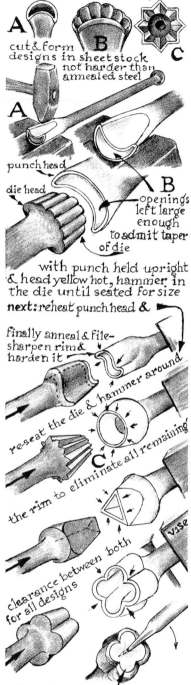

various patterned dies when forced into hot pre-shaped punch end openings & next sharpened & hardened, will

A cut & form designs in sheet stock not harder than annealed steel **B** **C**

punch head

die head

A

B openings left large enough to admit taper of die

with punch held upright & head yellow hot, hammer in the die until seated for size

next: reheat punch head &

finally anneal & file-sharpen rim & harden it

reseat the die & hammer around the rim to eliminate all remaining

C

clearance between both designs for all designs

vise

if punched-out discs get stuck in punch heads, pry them out with a pointed probe

or

press punch rim in candle wax beforehand, causing release of waste disc automatically, if inside cutting edge is polished mirror smooth

How to Forge Other Decorative Punches

If you want to add still more varieties of punches, using forging techniques rather than machining them will simplify the work.

Design A, for example, can be made by upsetting a head on a rod and drilling it out to a certain depth. Then place the hollow end in a swage with the hammer peen folding a portion of it, as shown. To finish the tool, simply sharpen the edge and harden it.

In *design B*, the die head is fluted by filing. Hammer the die head into the heated end of B, which has been shaped as in A. Once the end is heated, many light hammerblows on the outside of the punch will spread the heated steel and close the remaining gaps between the inner and outer die surfaces. It may take a few heatings to accomplish this. Be careful when you insert the male die that it is correctly seated before additional hammering begins. If the seating should be incorrect, an overlapping of indentations would ruin all the work that went before.

Design C is similar to the previous star pattern but, instead of having a thick wall of material, it relies on the spreading of the thin wall. Careful hammering with a narrow peen into the groove areas of the design will close up the spaces between them.

After finishing the shaping, sharpen the forged blanks, first with smooth files, then with rotating abrasive discs. If the die has exact and smooth surfaces the blank will not require machine- or hand-filing to improve it further. Temper the punch edges to the hardness of a cold chisel.

NOTE: Sharpening razor-sharp edges on punches that are meant to cut through metal follows the same principles that apply to cutting edges of wood-carving tools. Surprisingly, the sharpness of the cutting edge is more critical if *soft* materials are to be cut. The edges can be somewhat less precise if harder material is carved. If this is confusing to you, think of trying to cut through a cork with chisel and hammer. The cork simply *bends* under the tool without being cut. Cutting material involves a shearing action, not a tearing and bending action. This explanation should be a rule of thumb regarding tool cutting edges.

Punches to Cut through Soft Material

The illustration shows a machining technique for making the punch used to cut a clover-leaf design in soft material (felt, cloth, paper, for example). The interior of the punch can be drilled out.

When a beginner sees an expert doing the drilling he gets the impression that he, too, can do it easily. But the expert has learned through experience how to foresee possible errors and avoid repeating former mistakes. (See page 48, *Notes on Drilling*.)

The punch in the illustration must be drilled with a *leading pin* that prevents the drill from wandering. Slow down the rpm to prevent the drill from heating up.

First anneal the high-carbon punch head to its softest. Drill each new hole after filling the previous hole with a waste plug. Ram the plug into the finished hole so that the drilling of the next one will not be affected by the previous one. If the plug is not seated very tightly it may be necessary to drive deep punch marks around the plug edge to anchor it.

If successful in this operation, proceed with refining by grinding, filing, and sharpening as has been described in the making of other punches.

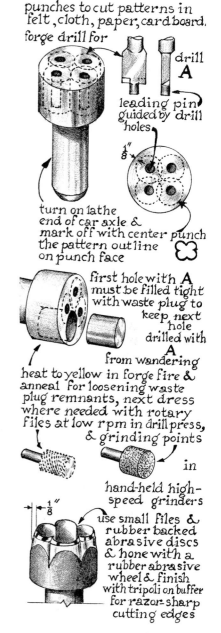

punches to cut patterns in felt, cloth, paper, cardboard. forge drill for

drill **A**

leading pin guided by drill holes.

$\frac{1}{8}''$

turn on lathe end of car axle & mark off with center punch the pattern outline on punch face

first hole with **A** must be filled tight with waste plug to keep next hole drilled with **A** from wandering

heat to yellow in forge fire & anneal for loosening waste plug remnants, next dress where needed with rotary files at low rpm in drill press, & grinding points in hand-held high-speed grinders

$\frac{1}{8}''$

use small files & rubber backed abrasive discs & hone with a rubber abrasive wheel & finish with tripoli on buffer for razor-sharp cutting edges

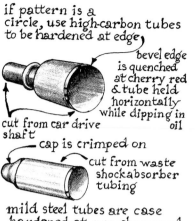

if pattern is a circle, use high-carbon tubes to be hardened at edge,

bevel edge is quenched at cherry red & tube held horizontally while dipping in oil

cut from car drive shaft

cap is crimped on

cut from waste shockabsorber tubing

mild steel tubes are case hardened at pre-sharpened cutting edges

Using Odds and Ends of Tubing for Punches

I have found that the drive shaft of a car, between the transmission and the differential, is made from a high-carbon steel tube welded at the seam. Because such drive shafts are quite large in diameter (in this case 2 5/8 inches), they are well suited for our purpose.

After cutting off an end section and leaving the stub shaft attached, all I needed to do was to refine the cutting edge on the lathe, sharpen it and temper it.

In tempering such a tool, see to it that 1/4 inch at the rim *gradually and evenly becomes cherry red*. At that point, holding the punch blank *horizontally*, quench it deeply and directly in oil, being sure to keep that horizontal position to avoid any danger of oil fume combustion. The danger is real if the piece is quenched in a vertical position, because if the air in the punch body is shut off from its surrounding the locked-up fumes of oil can become a combustible mixture with the trapped oxygen residue. The cherry red heat at the rim could possibly trigger an explosion just as a spark in a car engine explodes a combustible mixture.

Salvaged shock absorber tubing is another possible scrap source for punches. Unfortunately they are often made of mild steel, so it is necessary to case harden the cutting rims. Also a cap must fit tightly on the end of the tube to receive the hammerblows.

NOTES ON DRILLING

A drill press can feed a drill gently or forcefully; at low speed or high speed; using a small drill, a medium one, or a large one. These variables must be brought together in the correct combination if one is to succeed in a drilling job. In addition, it is important to know how *hard* the material to be drilled is.

Modern industry demands higher and higher speeds to cut most material, including steel. This naturally calls for cutting tools that can withstand breakage, overheating, wrong positioning of the tool, and a host of other factors that threaten to cause accidents or unsatisfactory results.

In my own shop I have reduced setbacks by *slowing down* all machinery in order to work with less danger, less heating-up of steel, and greater flexibility in tool alignment during these operations. In short, I propose that in learning to make do with what we have, we rely more on a clear understanding of what is involved during drilling, lathe turning, blacksmithing, and other shop activities and less on data geared to mass-production and precision fabrication.

Important Things to Remember about Drills

The standard twist drill has beveled cutting edges with both sides ground the same length and under the same angle so that the cutting edges automatically meet and seek the center of drill rotation.

Hand sharpening twist drills without the aid of a guiding instrument may leave cutting edges unsymmetrical. This will pull the drill outward, making it wander instead of seeking its own center of rotation. Once it tends to wander, eccentric forces are created, which often strain the drill to its breaking point.

From time to time during the sharpening, hold the drill before you in silhouette against a light background. Sight it to be sure that the sides are as near equal length as your skill can tell you.

11. Christmas Tree Candle Holders and Decorations

Punches can be used to make Christmas decorations from thin sheet metal. Tin cans that have a gold or silver sheen make good ornaments and, when kept indoors, will remain shiny year after year. Mine have lasted over thirty years and are as bright today as when I made them.

CHRISTMAS TREE CANDLE HOLDERS

These keep an upright position when hooked over a tree branch because they are weighted down by a little steel plug at the bottom. The farther the decorative element extends *below* the candle the more stable the upright position will be. Of course, the weighted part must stand free from surrounding branches.

The simplest way to fasten the weight plug into its seating hole is to strike the inserted plug with a heavy hammer on an anvil. The diameter then expands into the hole, locking the plug in place. This is a fastening method that comes in handy on many other occasions because it does away with precision work to keep plugs from falling out if the hole has only a moderate fit to start with.

After punching out the various elements for the candle holder, assemble them in a tight fit, soldering all the critical parts with regular tin solder. Since this is not much additional work, I would recommend that you do so for permanency.

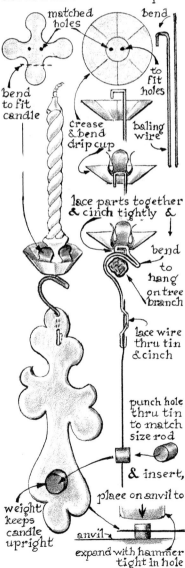

christmas tree ornaments & candle holders made from flattened food cans & waste industrial sheet steel strips

matched holes

bend

to fit holes

bend to fit candle

crease & bend drip cup

baling wire

lace parts together & cinch tightly &

bend to hang on tree branch

lace wire thru tin & cinch

punch hole thru tin to match size rod

& insert,

place on anvil to

weight keeps candle upright

anvil

expand with hammer tight in hole

49

OTHER DECORATIONS

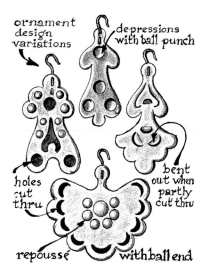

ornament design variations

depressions with ball punch

holes cut thru

repoussé

bent out when partly cut thru

with ball end

These can be made with the same tin can material or any other sheet metal you may find appealing. Keep in mind that punches for cutting through steel do not need to be absolutely razor sharp. If they are slightly dull, it introduces an element of surprise when the metal is punched on the rubber blanket glued on a stump. If the punch is slightly dull it merely *indents* the metal, leaving an interesting *low-relief* design. To make of this a *high-relief* pattern, turn the decoration over and use the repoussé technique of hammering a rounded punch into the depressions. These push the relief further outward.

Punches can also be used to cut only *partway* through the sheet. The cut section, bent outward, will catch and reflect light, adding sparkle to the decorations.

If you have enjoyed making the great variety of punches described in Chapter 10, you may want to gather friends together for a Christmas decoration "punching spree," as I have often done. The participants, sitting in front of the wooden stumps on the floor, can create beautiful designs as they share the variety of punches. The skill needed to use those tools can be acquired in minutes. And the decorations that result are well worth keeping.

12. Making Design Layouts for Punches

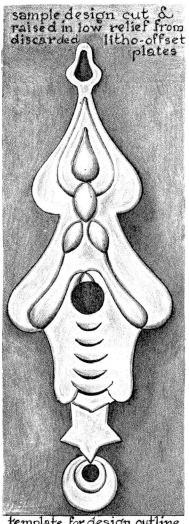

sample design cut & raised in low relief from discarded litho-offset plates

TRANSFERRING DESIGNS ONTO METAL

1) The design patterns for decorative articles can be drawn on paper and traced onto the metal with carbon paper.

2) Or, the paper on which the design is drawn can be rubbed with beeswax on the reverse side, then rubbed down onto the metal with a smooth, shallowly curved object (such as a tablespoon). If the metal is thin and soft, be careful not to bear down too hard. You may use a fingernail if the metal is fairly hard or heavy gauge. Following the outlines, use the various punches to cut through the paper and metal to free the piece. Finally, pull off the paper remnants.

3) Or, the pattern can be punched out of a transparent material, such as a sheet of acetate, using all the variety of punches you have. This sheet is then used as a template with which to draw the design onto the metal. In this way, a complete design can be laid out first and then cut with the same punches.

These methods make it unnecessary to scratch in the design with a sharp-pointed steel scribe, which can damage the metal if you miss the mark.

I offer here as examples several designs, but they are not necessarily to be copied. You will no doubt enjoy following your own imagination, no matter how elaborate the design may be. The wider your variety of punches, the greater will be your design possibilities.

Whether your design is elaborate or simple, you may want to combine the silhouettes with relief work made with the repoussé technique. Turning the sheet over, push the metal out, or make depressions on the original side, using the rounded tool ends made for that purpose. These hollow designs are very effective, looking like so many shining buttons. The combined raised and depressed patterns will give your design a three-dimensional character.

It is the leather worker, as a rule, who uses such repoussé and chasing punches on his material. For metalwork, the rubber blanket on the stump (as described in Chapter 10) acts as a good base when treating the metal in the same way.

template for design outline is made with the same pattern punches, in transparent acetate sheet

13. How to Make Miniature Chisels and Punches

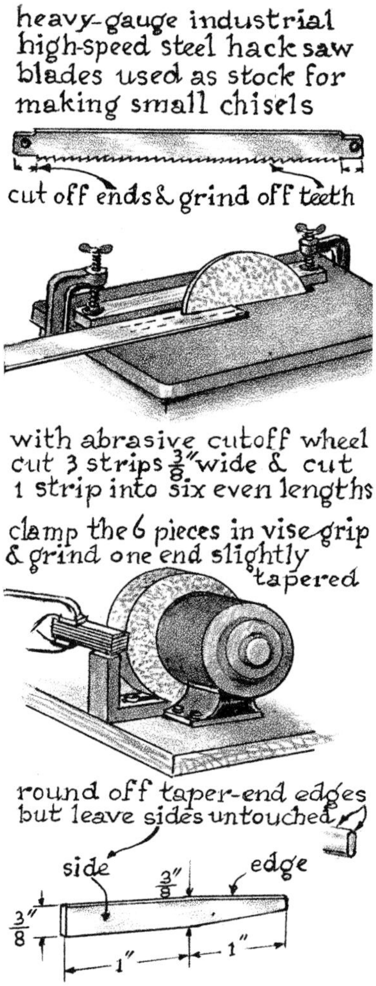

heavy-gauge industrial high-speed steel hack saw blades used as stock for making small chisels

cut off ends & grind off teeth

with abrasive cutoff wheel cut 3 strips ⅜″ wide & cut 1 strip into six even lengths

clamp the 6 pieces in vise grip & grind one end slightly tapered

round off taper-end edges but leave sides untouched

side   ⅜″   edge

⅜″

1″   1″

Miniature chisels and punches are needed when making a matrix and many small workpieces, for example, an escutcheon.

Used hacksaw blades can be very useful items that you may find discarded by industrial plants. They are generally made of high-speed tool steel. They are, as a rule, thick enough to be used as stock for small cutting tools such as miniature chisels and punches.

MAKING THE CHISEL BLADES

To cut up the blade, clamp a wood fence on the table of the abrasive cutoff wheel. Space it to cut six strips 3/8 inch wide from the blade. Hold the stack of six small pieces together with the visegrip plier.

Grind, as accurately as you can, a tapering end on this stack so that each is exactly the same as the others. From these make miniature chisels with different cutting edges. Fit the tapered end of each into a chisel-holder socket; it should be easy to insert or knock out the chisels so you can replace one with another when you want a different cutting edge.

MAKING THE CUTTING BLADE SOCKET

The holder is an annealed high-carbon steel bar or rod as shown. Drill a small hole in the end of the holder. Heat the holder end to a light *cherry red* and flatten it somewhat to match the width and thickness of the chisel's taper ending.

Heat the hollow flattened rod ending *yellow hot* and hammer in the taper end of the chisel, causing the hot steel to yield and seat the chisel taper. Then hammer the hot metal around the hard cold taper of the chisel until all surfaces contact one another exactly. The socket will now fit on such a taper as a lathe tailstock fits a Morse taper center.

SHAPING THE CUTTING ENDS

It is up to you to decide what shapes you wish to give the chisel cutting ends. The shaping is done in a simple forging action.

Note that high-speed tool steel, when heated *yellow hot*, can be bent into curves of your choice. But, unlike hot-forged high-carbon steel or mild steel, it will resist peening or upsetting. High-speed tool steel has been designed to maintain considerable hardness even when heated; it is only at *light yellow* heat that it will yield to bending. And once it is cooled without quenching or tempering it will return to its original hardness.

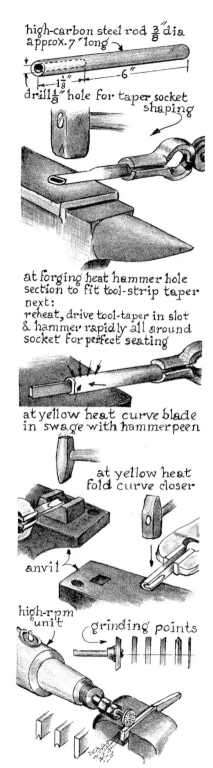

high-carbon steel rod ⅜" dia approx. 7" long

drill ⅛" hole for taper socket shaping

at forging heat hammer hole section to fit tool-strip taper
next:
reheat, drive tool-taper in slot & hammer rapidly all around socket for perfect seating

at yellow heat curve blade in swage with hammer peen

at yellow heat fold curve closer

anvil

high-rpm unit   grinding points

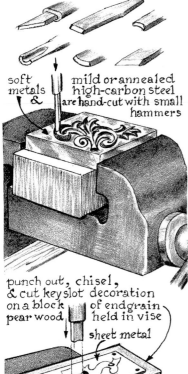

useful cutting ends shaped
with hand-held high-r.p.m.unit

soft
metals
&
mild or annealed
high-carbon steel
are hand-cut with small
hammers

punch out, chisel,
& cut key slot decoration
on a block
pear wood
of endgrain
held in vise
sheet metal

when using steel $\frac{1}{2}$" thick
or over, cut pattern with
abrasive cut-off wheel

I have always gone by this rule of thumb: After heating and then cooling, high-speed tool steel will cut any partially annealed regular high-carbon steel satisfactorily and any well annealed high-carbon steel and mild steel easily.

MAKING AN ESCUTCHEON

Transfer the design onto a piece of sheet metal of your choice. It should be annealed steel or annealed silver, brass, aluminum, or any other metal of comparable softness.

The self-explanatory illustrations show step by step drilling, shearing, punching, filing, grinding, buffing.

Cutting with chisels and punches is best done on a base of endgrain fruitwood clamped in the vise, as shown. The sharper the tool edges, the fewer difficulties you will meet.

When keyholes require exact patterned contours, smooth files, especially in small sizes such as locksmiths use, will serve best.

It is in these small projects that you can apply your acquired skill in making your own files, especially if you must reach small spaces for the cross section design you need.

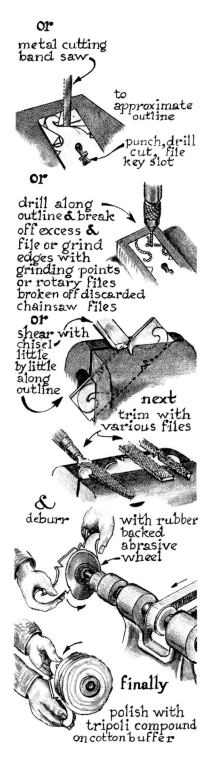

or

metal cutting band saw

to approximate outline

punch, drill cut, file key slot

or

drill along outline & break off excess & file or grind edges with grinding points or rotary files broken off discarded chainsaw files

or

shear with chisel little by little along outline

next trim with various files

&

deburr

with rubber backed abrasive wheel

finally

polish with tripoli compound on cotton buffer

14. A Punch to Cut Small Washers from a Metal Strip

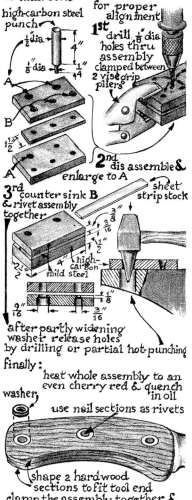

making a punch-jig to cut small washers from thin strips of brass or mild steel

high-carbon steel punch

for proper alignment

1st drill ⅛" dia holes thru assembly clamped between 2 vise grip pliers

½" dia

4"

1¼"

⅛" dia

A

B

1½"

A

2nd dis assemble & enlarge to A

3rd counter sink **B** & rivet assembly together

sheet strip stock

⅜"

³⁄₁₆"

½"

4" high-carbon mild steel

²⁄₅

¹⁄₈"

⁹⁄₁₆"

³⁄₁₆"

after partly widening washer release holes by drilling or partial hot-punching

finally: heat whole assembly to an even cherry red & quench in oil

washer

use nail sections as rivets

shape 2 hardwood sections to fit tool end clamp the assembly together & drill the rivet holes thru

Brass washers can be used to rivet wood onto the steel handles of knives, cleavers, wood-carving tools, fireplace tools, and others. The color of the wood, the color of the washer, and the color of the rivet will all be different, enhancing the appearance of the handles.

Turn the punch on a metal-turning lathe and temper it to the hardness of a cold chisel. Follow the sequence in the illustrations, being careful to maintain correct alignment of punch and guide hole in the riveted assembly. If all has been carried out successfully, the brass stock fed into the jig and then punch-cut will easily produce small, clean-cut brass washers.

ASSEMBLING A HANDLE WITH THE WASHERS

If you do not want the washers and the rivet heads to protrude from the wood surface, you must first countersink the washers themselves before imbedding them into countersunk depressions in the wood. The washer countersinking is done with a center punch. This may be a novelty to some craftsmen but is much simpler than doing it with a countersink drill.

Just place the washer on an endgrain wood stump, put the center-punch in the washer hole, and hammer it down. This leaves a slightly bent cup shape in the washer. When all parts are assembled for riveting, the rivet head will fill the washer cup depression completely.

The washers are seated with a small countersink cutter that has a pilot pin to keep it from wandering.

Use files, abrasive discs, and polishers to smooth the surface of the wooden handle. This will bring out the contrasting colors of wood, washer, and rivet head.

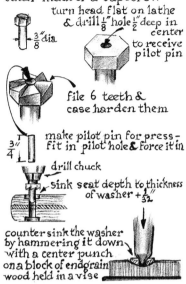

next:
counter sink washer seats with cutter made of a capscrew

turn head flat on lathe & drill $\frac{1}{8}$" hole $\frac{1}{2}$" deep in center to receive pilot pin

$\frac{3}{8}$" dia

file 6 teeth & case harden them

make pilot pin for press-fit in pilot hole & force it in

$\frac{3}{4}$"

drill chuck

sink seat depth to thickness of washer + $\frac{1}{32}$"

counter sink the washer by hammering it down with a center punch on a block of endgrain wood held in a vise

15. Makeshift Bearings

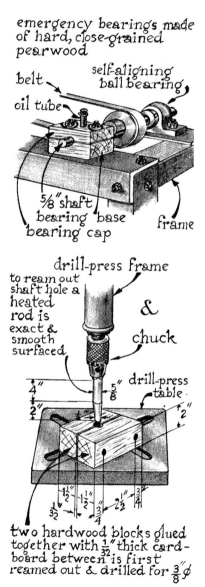

emergency bearings made of hard, close-grained pearwood

belt

self-aligning ball bearing

oil tube

5/8" shaft

bearing base

bearing cap

frame

to ream out shaft hole a heated rod is exact & smooth surfaced

drill-press frame

&

chuck

drill-press table

4"

5/8"

2"

1/2"

1 1/2"   1 1/4"   2 1/2"   3/4"

1/32   1/2   3/4

two hardwood blocks glued together with 1/32" thick cardboard between is first reamed out & drilled for 3/8"∅

MAKING A BEARING OUT OF WOOD

If a bearing breaks down in the shop and if you are located very far from stores where they are sold, you can make one out of wood.

First Step

Choose a dry branch of fruitwood from orchard prunings or some comparable fine-grained wood that has the closest grain possible. As a rule, pearwood is best. Cut from it two blocks and glue them together with thin cardboard in between. Bolt this block onto the location of the bearing that is to be replaced. Mark off the exact center of the hole to be drilled through the wood to fit the shaft.

Drill the hole *slightly undersized* at first but as well aligned with the axis of rotation of the shaft as possible.

Second Step

Use a steel rod the size of the shaft and taper it gently so that the small size of the taper fits in the predrilled, undersized hole. Place the block on the table of the drill press and put the tapered rod in the drill chuck to test the setup. When you are satisfied that all is ready, remove the tapered rod and heat it in the forge fire to the point that it will scorch wood.

Quickly transfer the rod to the drill chuck and burn it through the wood, making sure that the heat is not so great that the smoke combusts into flame. The heating does two things: momentarily it *softens* the wood; and, while it scorches, makes the final surface of the hole exact, smooth, and hard.

If all has gone well and the block barely fits onto the shaft, grease the hole and let the shaft run into it with its tight fit. The grease, upon heating, will penetrate the wood.

Third Step

After the bolt holes have been drilled, split the block in two along the cardboard. The top part of the block is the *bearing cap.*

Drill the bolt holes with some clearance, so that you can make a slight adjustment in the placement of the bearing if necessary. If, in assembling, you find that the shaft hole is still too tight, placing thin shims between the bearing cap and bearing pillow will eliminate the friction. Provide the bearing with a lubrication hole and groove.

When installing the bearing, spin the shaft freehand and you will notice immediately whether or not the bearing is well aligned and if adjustments are called for.

Such a bearing will stand up under regular use for a long time. I have used one in my own shop for years.

Adjustments

If the bearing is too low, you may have to place below it strips of thin metal in the pattern of its footing, with the holes corresponding to the bolts. Or if, on the other hand, it is too high, plane or sand off enough wood to lower the bearing to the correct height.

The thickness of the cardboard must be made up for with two shims of wood or metal of that same thickness. If that is a little too thick, try progressively thinner shims until the bolted-down cap does not bind onto the rotating shaft. The shim's edge should just touch the rotating shaft.

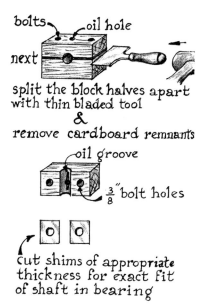

bolts   oil hole

next

split the block halves apart with thin bladed tool
&
remove cardboard remnants

oil groove

$\frac{3}{8}$" bolt holes

cut shims of appropriate thickness for exact fit of shaft in bearing

USING DISCARDED BALL BEARINGS

Electrical motor and automotive repair shops quite often discard noisy ball bearings; some are from burned-out motors and are hardly worn at all. If proprietors of such shops are sympathetic with your efforts, they will let you rummage through their scrap barrels. You will be surprised how often you will find unexpected treasures in addition to the things you are looking for.

Bearing shaft holes that are slightly too large

Often you can locate a thin-walled tube that fits over the shaft but may be a little too thick to fit within the bearing hole. Slip the tube section onto a tight-fitting wooden rod and clamp it in the lathe chuck or the drill press chuck. Turn or grind down a small section of that outer tube surface, testing the bearing over it for a fit. If that section is left to taper outward somewhat it will act as a wedge between the bearing opening and the shaft diameter. In assembly, you can tap it into the space it is to fill between bearing and shaft.

After assembly, clamp a little collar onto the shaft to hold the protruding section of the tube shim in position.

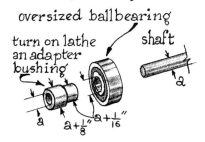

scrapped ball bearings as emergency replacement

oversized ballbearing

turn on lathe an adapter bushing   shaft

a   a

a+$\frac{1}{8}$"   a+$\frac{1}{16}$"

assembled in wooden
bearing housing

bushing
set screw
a

bearing base

collar &
set screw
hold bushing
in place

grinding outer bearing race
to fit template

hard coarse
power
wheel

shoulder washers
let outer race
spin freely

hands
steadied
on bench

template hole

bearing cap

bearing cap
clamps on the
outer ball race
(after bearing &
shaft assembly)
absorbing
possible unaligned
shaft-bearing block
positioning

How to install the ball bearing

The illustration shows the wooden pillow block that holds down the ball bearing. Since the wood in this instance is not used as a bearing itself but simply as a seat for the ball bearing, the wood can be hard-grained; it need not be close-grained. Oak, maple, or ash will do.

After the height of the bearing has been determined and the whole assembly has been positioned, do not cinch the hold-down bolts until you are certain that the ball bearing itself is perfectly aligned with the shaft. This will protect the ball races from wearing at their sides.

NOTE: The outer ball races in self-aligning ball bearings have spherical outer surfaces representing the central section of a sphere measuring the width of such an outer ball race. Examine a self-aligning ball bearing in a ball bearing supply store, if the three-dimensional aspect of the spherical outer surface of the bearing is too difficult to visualize from drawn illustration.

In the case of these you do not need to make the surface of the bearing seat spherical. The illustration shows that a two-part *cylindrical seating* can be clamped onto the approximate spherical outer race in a test run. This allows the spherical surface of the outer race to seek its own aligned position just before the bearing seating is clamped down onto the ball bearing.

Grinding the Spherical Surface of the Outer Ball Race

Cut a template with a circular opening the size of the outer diameter of the outer ball race. Fit a wooden rod tightly into the ball bearing. Cut two cardboard discs with central holes to fit snugly on the wooden rod. These discs are to keep abrasive dust from entering the vital parts of the ball bearing; they are placed on each side of the ball bearing with thick grease in between. The discs do not interfere with the spinning of the *outer* race.

Holding the assembly in both hands, move the outer race into contact with a rotating hard and coarse grinding wheel. The ball bearing race, spun by the wheel, is at the same time being ground down. Aim to grind the steel while it rotates at maximum effectiveness by slanting it, as shown.

The grinding job can be called finished when the outer bearing race can slip through that hole, evenly touching the portion of the circle in the template.

NOTE: The foregoing methods of improvising makeshift bearings to replace broken ones are only two of the many possibilities one can inventively resort to in an emergency.

16. Making Accessory Tools for the Wood-Turning Lathe

If your shop has a wood-turning lathe, and also an assortment of machine tools, you can easily use this lathe to drive implements designed for other uses. Grinding wheels or sanding discs can be mounted on the lathe headstock and driven by the lathe. This is an ideal adaptation because the step pulley on the lathe headstock allows for various speeds; you should use the fastest speed for small wheels, the slowest speed for as big a wheel as the lathe will take.

A long grinding arbor makes room for such hand-held instruments as a reverse lathe unit, which facilitates the regrinding of engine valves. But it also provides much needed room when awkward-shaped articles have to be ground. Extra sturdy, precisely fitting arbors must be securely clamped in the headstock to prevent the vibration of high rpm small grinding wheels.

Very small, worn-down abrasive cutoff wheels work ideally on the wood-turning lathe when you need to do an engine valve regrinding job. Use the method shown in the illustration.

Hand hold a small reverse lathe unit, keeping both hands steadied against the lathe bed. Align the bevel of the valve with the side surface of the cutoff wheel remnant; the grinding job is finished in a fraction of a minute. In this way twelve valves of a six-cylinder car engine can be reground to perfection in no time.

Note that the illustrations show an arrangement made in my own shop to suit my particular needs. Inventiveness and resourcefulness play a major role in using recycled material from an often maligned junk pile. This points up once again how much sense it makes to build up a stock of scrap steel and salvaged objects: you will become better and better equipped as time goes on. Thus "making tools to make tools" should become more and more the norm of daily activity.

If you live in or near rural areas you probably have access to the fruit tree prunings stacked around an orchard. These fruitwood branches make excellent stock from which to make small tool handles. The farmer in my area is generally sympathetic with my needs when I explain to him that I am a practicing artist-craftsman. When I offer him some picture postcards of my work, he usually permits me in exchange to help myself to his prunings.

I have designed a jig to round off the end of a wooden handle and at the same time to leave a seating hole in the center to receive the tool's tang.

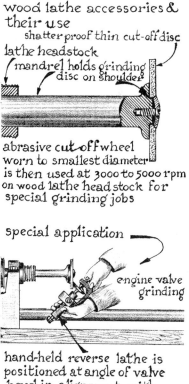

wood lathe accessories & their use

shatter proof thin cut-off disc
lathe headstock
mandrel holds grinding disc on shoulder

abrasive cut-off wheel worn to smallest diameter is then used at 3000 to 5000 rpm on wood lathe head stock for special grinding jobs

special application

engine valve grinding

hand-held reverse lathe is positioned at angle of valve bevel in alignment with wheel's side, which, upon contact, spin-grinds precisely a new & smooth final bevel surface texture

a handle cutter-head fastened in wood lathe head-stock is to spin at approx. 1750 rpm to cut hand-held branch

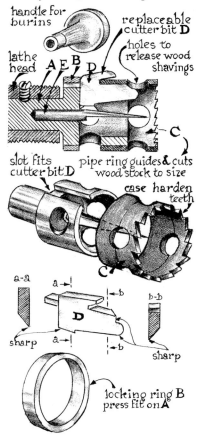

cutter is made on metal-turning lathe from a car axle section

bevel

drill hole for leading pin for a snug fit

bevel

grind one side of pin flat to cut the wood while pin's round side keeps wood from wandering

bevel, pin's filed-in teeth are to be tempered dark bronze

pin can be knocked out when needed

pin makes the preliminary seat for the tool tang, which is to be burned in

turning wood handles for small tools in a cutter designed for limited quantity production using a simple homeshop lathe

handle for burins

replaceable cutter bit **D**

holes to release wood shavings

lathe head **A E B D**

— C

slot fits cutter bit D

pipe ring guides & cuts wood stock to size

case harden teeth

C

a-a
a →
← b
b-b

D

sharp   a →   ← b   sharp

locking ring B press fit on A

Without a guiding pin, there is a danger that the stock ending may wander at the point of engagement with the cutter's teeth. This will happen if you have extracted the guide pin because you do not want a tang hole in a wood ending. In this case, bevel the wood edge so that it will slip inside the jig about a quarter of an inch. The stock can then be safely fed freehand with the tailscrew.

AN ADJUSTABLE CUTTER TO MAKE SMALL WOODEN HANDLES

I contoured cutter element D in such a fashion that I could slip it into a slot while the ring-guide B and cutter C would hold it snugly in the jig assembly.

Examine the illustration carefully. It clearly shows the locked-up position of D during the cutting action. Element C, though fitting snugly on A, does not fit so tightly that it could not be knocked off should you wish to make D interchangeable with a cutter element of a different profile.

The side holes in both jig body A and cutter ring C simply serve as escape gates for the wood pulp that is thrown out centrifugally during the high-speed cutting action.

Element E is simply a cutting pin, which can be inserted tightly in the main body A so that a tang hole can be cut into the small handle. At the same time, that pin will act as an alignment guide to prevent any wandering of the workpiece during the cutting action.

The illustrations show the jig and wood stock held and fed by the tailstock center and kept from turning by the clamped-on visegrip pliers.

The craftsman who has become increasingly skilled in making things to fill his needs is offered in the foregoing an approach to designing and making a new tool. In my own experience, I have found that dexterous people seem to be endowed also with a good measure of inventiveness, which enables them to design and construct whatever accessories may be useful to them. In this way they gain ever greater independence and freedom to earn their livelihood in a unique and individual manner.

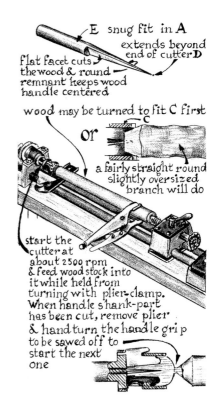

E snug fit in A
extends beyond end of cutter D
flat facet cuts the wood & round remnant keeps wood handle centered

wood may be turned to fit C first

or

a fairly straight round slightly oversized branch will do

start the cutter at about 2500 rpm & feed wood stock into it while held from turning with plier-clamp. When handle shank-part has been cut, remove plier & hand turn the handle grip to be sawed off to start the next one

17. Wire-Straightening Tools

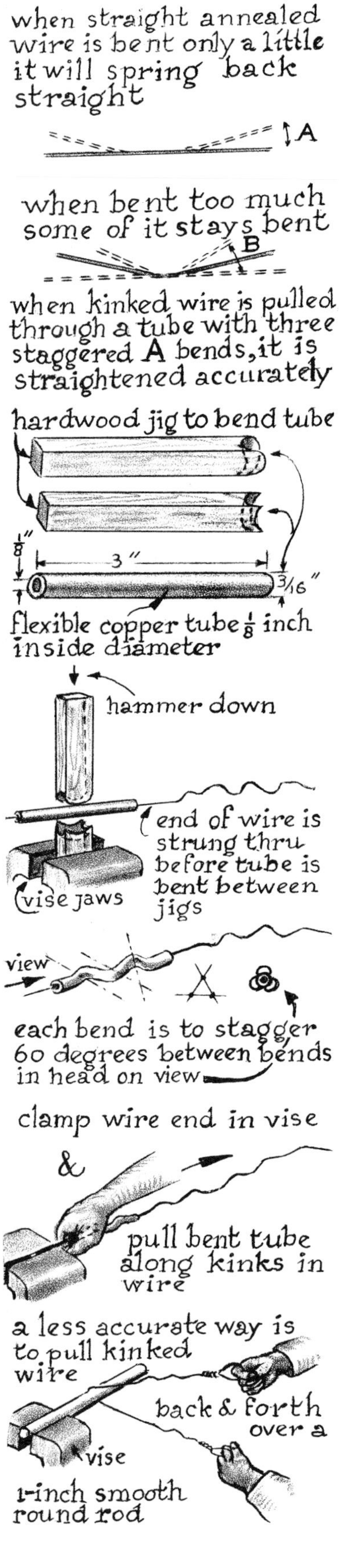

when straight annealed wire is bent only a little it will spring back straight

A

when bent too much some of it stays bent

B

when kinked wire is pulled through a tube with three staggered A bends, it is straightened accurately

hardwood jig to bend tube

$\frac{1}{8}$"
3"
$\frac{3}{16}$"

flexible copper tube $\frac{1}{8}$ inch inside diameter

hammer down

end of wire is strung thru before tube is bent between jigs

vise jaws

view

each bend is to stagger 60 degrees between bends in head on view

clamp wire end in vise

&

pull bent tube along kinks in wire

a less accurate way is to pull kinked wire

back & forth over a

vise

1-inch smooth round rod

Coils of old kinky wire can often be quickly and easily straightened with a jig.

THE FIRST JIG

Slip the end of the twisted wire through a small copper tube bent as shown in the illustrations. Clamp a short protruding end of the wire between the vise jaws, or loop it around a fixed anchor point, and pull the bent tube along the full length of the wire. This will straighten it completely. The diagrams explain what happens.

It is awkward to reuse the tube because it is difficult to manipulate another wire ending through it *after* it has been bent. For this reason, a second type of jig is more versatile.

THE SECOND JIG

Cut three sections from a hexagonal bar and drill a small hole through each one. It is important to make the hole just barely large enough to let the wire slide through.

Round off the holes at both ends to allow the bent wire to slip by without being cut on its way through. Ample lubrication during the pulling will also smooth the process of unbending the wire.

The jig housing is made as illustrated to hold the three hexagonal sections.

After the wire ending has been laced through each section separately, insert them in the housing in a staggered position. This easy assembly eliminates the problem of threading the wire through as must be done in the first method. The grip latch on the housing makes it convenient for the instrument to be pulled with great force, should that be necessary.

Keep in mind that straightening wire can only be done in this way if the wire is not too thick or if it is not made of spring steel.

It should go without saying that a tool such as this one is useful only if the wire to be recycled is in good enough condition to be salvaged at all.

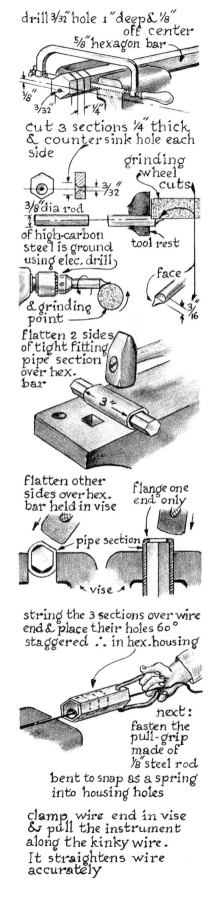

drill 3/32" hole 1" deep & 1/8" off center

5/8" hexagon bar

1/8" 3/32" 1/4"

cut 3 sections 1/4" thick & countersink hole each side

3/32"

3/8" dia rod

grinding wheel cuts

of high-carbon steel is ground using elec. drill

tool rest

& grinding point

face 3/16"

flatten 2 sides of tight fitting pipe section over hex. bar

flatten other sides over hex. bar held in vise

flange one end only

pipe section

vise

string the 3 sections over wire end & place their holes 60° staggered ∴ in hex. housing

next: fasten the pull-grip made of 1/8" steel rod bent to snap as a spring into housing holes

clamp wire end in vise & pull the instrument along the kinky wire. It straightens wire accurately

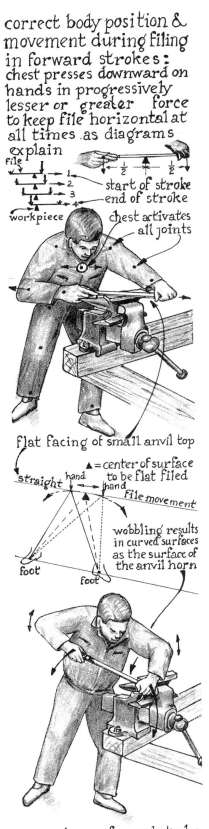

correct body position &
movement during filing
in forward strokes:
chest presses downward on
hands in progressively
lesser or greater force
to keep file horizontal at
all times as diagrams
explain

file

1
2
3
4
start of stroke
end of stroke
workpiece
chest activates
all joints

flat facing of small anvil top

▲ = center of surface
to be flat filed
straight hand
hand
File movement

wobbling results
in curved surfaces
as the surface of
the anvil horn

foot

foot

press down on forward stroke
but let only weight of file
slide over work piece surface
on return stroke

18. Flat Filing and Drilling

Leonardo da Vinci designed a machine to cut file serrations automatically. This made it possible for others to improve filing techniques in the centuries that followed; during the age of steam engines, craftsmen learned to file with a precision that matched the machine-tool accuracy of later years. The stress was on learning to file flat surfaces to an absolute perfection. One could say that the craft of *flat filing* is the hallmark of the completion of the machinist's training.

THE PROPER USE OF THE FILE

The illustration shows the proper stance for flat filing. In this case, a small, well-annealed anvil face is to be filed perfectly flat.

The worker's leading foot is placed in the direction of the file stroke and the other foot is placed far enough away to steady his position. This makes it possible for him to move his body backward and forward through the hip, knee and ankle joints just enough to keep pace with the backward and forward movements of the hands holding the file.

The beginner should aim to hold the file in a position perfectly parallel with the horizontal surface to be flat filed. He must learn to bear down on the forward stroke of the file and release all downward pressure on the return stroke.

Soon he will become aware that it is the movements of his *whole body*, not just of his arm and hand, that must combine for accuracy and effectiveness. From then on repeated practice is required to eliminate the initial wobbling motion that every beginner experiences. Examine the diagrams carefully to visualize what actually takes place.

EQUIPMENT

The items listed are the tools I was provided with during my first year at the college of Marine Engineering in Groningen, Holland, in 1916. They are still the basic ones used today. Half the course time was devoted to shop training. The first six months were spent learning the art of flat filing. Next came blacksmithing. The remaining time was spent on applying what had been learned to make actual steam engine parts. Hand skills were combined with learning how to use the basic machine tools: the drill press, metal-turning lathe, and shaper.

In this school, all equipment was old and fairly dilapidated. That required still more skill on the part of the student if he was to carry out his assignments and meet the final test requirements for accuracy. In those years it was absolutely necessary in the event of a mid-ocean breakdown that the marine engineer on board ship be able to repair, in the ship's machine shop, the engine with sufficient skill and know-how to allow the ship at least to limp into port under its own steam for more permanent repairs. The skills I acquired in those early years have been a boon to me all my life. Many times have hand skills at their best saved the situation when only a minimum of equipment was available.

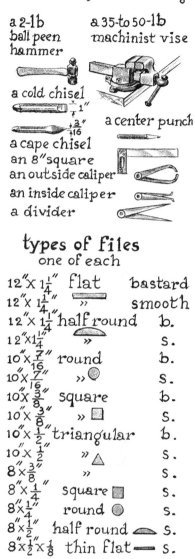

needed equipment to carry out assignments in learning flat filing

a 2-lb ball peen hammer   a 35-to 50-lb machinist vise

a cold chisel $\frac{1}{4}$"   a center punch

$\frac{3}{16}$"

a cape chisel
an 8" square
an outside caliper
an inside caliper
a divider

types of files
one of each

12"x 1$\frac{1}{4}$" flat		bastard
12"x 1$\frac{1}{4}$" "		smooth
12"x 1$\frac{1}{4}$" half round		b.
12"x1$\frac{1}{4}$" "		s.
10"x$\frac{7}{16}$" round		b.
10"x$\frac{7}{16}$" "		s.
10"x$\frac{3}{8}$" square		b.
10"x$\frac{3}{8}$" "		s.
10"x$\frac{1}{2}$" triangular		b.
10"x$\frac{1}{2}$" "		s.
8"x$\frac{3}{8}$" "		s.
8"x$\frac{1}{4}$" square		s.
8"x$\frac{1}{4}$" round		s.
8"x$\frac{1}{2}$" half round		s.
8"x$\frac{1}{2}$"x$\frac{1}{8}$ thin flat		s.

a surface gauge or a part that has been machined flat as a drill press table or a circular saw;- planer table

some soot & shellac to blacken surfaces for scribe marking and some salvaged litho-offset ink for testing the accuracy of flat filed surfaces on surface gauges

flat filing exercises
1ˢᵗ assignment
file all sides of a bar 1/16″ less

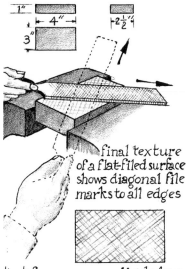

final texture
of a flat-filed surface
shows diagonal file
marks to all edges

test for accuracy: jiggle bar
on machined table gauge that
has been blackened a little & next
move bar over table to reveal
low & high spots

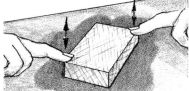

after 1ˢᵗ accurate flat surface
file its opposite flat & parallel.
calipers must lightly "feel" total
surface evenly for all sides
up to   edges

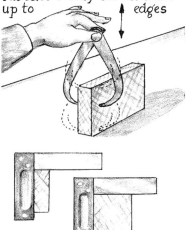

all sides must be filed 90°
to each other, checked on
surface gauge & with calipers
for parallelity

HOW TO LEARN FLAT FILING

From the easiest assignment to the most difficult one, the student will gradually develop increasing skill in flat filing. Cumulatively this enables him to compete with the machine in accuracy. Perseverance and self-discipline will carry him through. It did so for the thousands before us who had to make do with a minimum of machine help.

First Assignment

Cut from a hot-rolled mild steel bar a piece 3 inches wide, 1 inch thick, and 4 inches long. Clamp it in the vise in a horizontal position and proceed as shown. Sometimes a new piece of hot-rolled steel has a hard scale that could possibly damage the sharp file teeth. If you find that this is the case, it would be wise to hack off the scale with a sharp chisel. Cut off only a thin sliver, being careful that at no time does the chisel cut deeper than necessary. Once the surface has been scaled, the file can be used without the danger of becoming dulled.

As soon as the cold chisel marks have been filed away, put the surface to the first test for flatness on a surface gauge. A flat machined part in the shop will serve well for a gauge.

Rub into its surface a little lampblack and grease mixture, wiping off all excess. Sliding the filed surface over it will show, by the black spots left on it, the degree of accuracy that has been reached and will indicate where corrections must be made.

After total surface accuracy has been achieved and demonstrated with the surface gauge, replace the *bastard file* with the smooth file. The final smooth surface must pass the test for absolute accuracy.

It is at this point that, with gained skill, you can file the opposite side, which then must be tested with the caliper instead of the surface gauge. The caliper, finely adjusted to barely touch the steel, will make it possible for you to *feel* where corrective filing is needed.

After tests show accuracy, the remaining sides of the block can be filed in the same way. One additional test must then be made. The square will show whether all sides meet at exactly 90 degrees.

Place the square over the edges of the block and hold it up against the light. Any inaccuracy will show up as a light leak, indicating where corrective filing must be done.

When the workpiece has been completed, there is no doubt that you will have quite a few blisters on your hands to show for your efforts, but you can now face more complicated assignments with greater confidence.

The steps described in the first assignment are all applicable in what is to follow. Each successive project is designed to exercise and utilize your acquired abilities.

Second Assignment

Once the 1 by 1 by 4-inch bar has been filed, mark off with a scribe a slot location and accent it with small center-punch marks about 1/4 inch apart placed on the scribed lines. This ensures that the slot location will remain visible even when extended work is done on that surface.

Use a cape chisel to precut the slot within the marked lines to a depth just under the given measurement. A follow-up filing into the slot can be done accurately without danger of overshooting our aim. It is necessary, nonetheless, to file cautiously and accurately.

Making a key to fit the slot. Forge a key blank (an outmoded design) somewhat larger than would fit the slot. File it down to correct size. Probing will indicate where corrective filing must be done. During corrective filing one must learn how to hold or slant the file in such a way that local areas only can be filed without touching surrounding areas in order to correct inaccuracies. Often using the tip of the file only will reduce local spots to needed size.

Third Assignment

This assignment repeats the second one with the added complication that each of the four slots measured with the caliper must show that its opposite slot bottom runs parallel and that all are equidistant. All four slots must furthermore fit the same key evenly when the key is tapped snugly through the slots with the back of a hammer stem. The key should still hold the slot in the last 1/8 inch of its travel. When the piece is held up against the light for that last 1/8 inch fit, a slight glimmer, if any, should show evenly between contacting sides.

Fourth Assignment: Drilling

The drill press is used in this project. First check the proper sized drill for accurate alignment. Clamp it in the drill chuck and rotate it momentarily under power to test it for perfect central alignment. Since most modern drill presses have three-jawed chucks, see to it that the drill shank has been inserted as far as it will go in order to intercept any possible wobble.

Old-fashioned drills have Morse taper endings that fit Morse taper drill seatings. That system eliminated all possible wobble of the drill. Modern three-jawed drill chucks, however, have been machine perfected to such an extent that cylindrical drill shanks can be accurately aligned and held fast effectively.

Since it is cheaper to manufacture drills with cylindrical shanks, and the three-jawed chuck can take all sizes of drills, the modern system has replaced almost entirely the old-fashioned taper shank drill.

Adjust the drill press table to its desired height. Place the workpiece on it and lower the drill so that its point fits exactly in the previously made centerpunch mark on the workpiece. Hold it in that position momentarily and, with whatever means is available, clamp the workpiece to the drill press table securely.

Position the drill up and down to make sure that the correct centering and aligning has not gone awry during this "make ready." (The term *make ready* is used in all trades that require a dry run before actual cutting, punching, printing begins.) Even then the first real cut with the drill must be closely watched so that a corrective step can be applied immediately.

Sometimes the corrective step involves giving the drill press table a gentle sideways tap with the back of a hammer stem, or the workpiece on the drill press table might require a gentle tap in whatever direction to ensure that all is centrally secured. Such adjustments will make the drill cut correctly before it goes much deeper.

In this progressive fashion, it is possible to drill holes precisely in marked-off locations. A test with the caliper afterward will check on the accuracy of the end result.

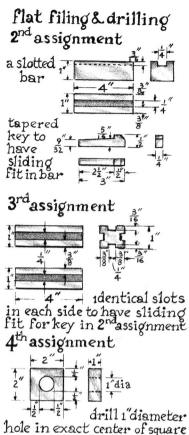

flat filing & drilling
2nd assignment
a slotted bar

tapered key to have sliding fit in bar

3rd assignment

4" identical slots in each side to have sliding fit for key in 2nd assignment

4th assignment

drill 1" diameter hole in exact center of square & measure with caliper at each side for accuracy

WARNING: If a workpiece has been clamped on the drill press table so that the drill will be aligned with the hole in the table, the final cut will make the thin steel remaining at the bottom bend outward the moment the drill begins to emerge below. The thin steel then bends away and, instead of being cut by the drill, the edges begin to bind under progressively increasing strain. It is therefore necessary that you develop the ability to "feel" and "hear" telltale signs of binding. Once you notice them, immediately reduce the downward pressure of the drill to relieve the strain on it should it be slightly dull. Otherwise its outside cutting edge will begin to *rub* instead of *cut*, generating heat and endangering the temper hardness of a high-carbon steel drill.

All this can be prevented if you clamp the workpiece on a flat piece of waste steel. This allows the drill to cut cleanly all the way through solid steel.

Fifth Assignment

Scribe off a hexagon around the hole and tangent to it. Two of its sides should run parallel to the sides of the workpiece. Make precise center-punch marks on each corner of the scribed hexagon. Duplicate this procedure on the other side of the workpiece.

Next, file each side of the hexagon with a bastard file, keeping the hexagon slightly undersized. Constant checking of each side with calipers will reveal well in advance what corrective filing will be required. Follow up with a smooth file to *refine* the surface textures, stopping short of an absolute final dimension.

When you reach this point, stop and switch to making a hexagonal bar, as illustrated in the sixth assignment. This bar must be made to fit in the hexagonal hole. Once made, return to where you left off in the fifth assignment and test the fit between the hexagonal bar and the hole. This will indicate whether the 120-degree angles at which the sides must meet are exact. (A template can be cut with a single exact 120-degree angle. It will serve during the making and testing of the two workpieces.)

As the final test check that the bar has an even sliding fit from the moment it is inserted into the hole until the last 1/8 inch of travel. At that point only a small glimmer of light should be visible at the sides of the hexagon.

Remove the bar and tumble it 60 degrees. Insert it in the hole again and test it as before; repeat the 60-degree turn until the original position has been reestablished.

If you have successfully passed this test, the seventh and eighth assignments are within reach of your ability. The illustrations of these assignments should now be self-explanatory.

No additional assignments will be described although my past training carried me through many more. This gave me the ability to do three-dimensional projects with perfect sliding fits.

Trained in this way, any craftsman could fabricate from the ground up most parts of a steam engine; a complete crankshaft bearing head; piston rod bearing ends; sliding steam valves; speed regulator hinges; and similar projects.

I hope that not only eager students, but also dedicated teachers will have the desire to revive old-fashioned methods in teaching handcrafts, including flat filing at its best.

5ᵗʰ assignment
file precise a hexagon hole in center of square
← 2″ →

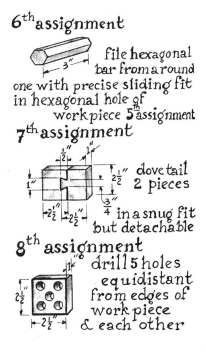

6ᵗʰ assignment
file hexagonal bar from a round one with precise sliding fit in hexagonal hole of workpiece 5ᵗʰ assignment
← 3″ →

7ᵗʰ assignment
dove tail 2 pieces
in a snug fit but detachable

8ᵗʰ assignment
drill 5 holes equidistant from edges of work piece & each other

19. Files, Rasps, and Grindstones

cleaning & reconditioning dirty & worn files

bear down hard

brass strip

copper sheet inserts

dirty file

wood block prop

brass strip teeth dislodge metal pulp

battery acid 24 hrs.

BATTERY

worn files

1 hr. water rinse

plastic tray

Old files, thrown out because they are too worn, frequently come our way. Their excellent high-carbon tool steel can be used as stock for making high-quality gouges and other cutting tools.

Before forging files into tool blanks, grind off the teeth. This will eliminate the danger of the steel cracking where serrations remain.

HOW TO CLEAN DIRTY BUT SHARP FILES

If metal pulp clogs the file's serrations, it can be dislodged with steel wire brushes made for that purpose. A disadvantage in using a brush is that its hard steel tines compete with the file's own hardness. This tends to reduce the sharpness of the file, as well as its lifetime. If you do use a brush, it should be one with *brass* tines, which will not wear down the steel teeth of the file appreciably.

My preference is to use a strip of brass or even mild steel measuring 1 inch by 8 inches by 1/16 inch, instead of a brush. Press it on the file surface, moving it parallel to the serrations. The file will automatically cut teeth in the brass strip, and these in turn can reach the bottom of the file grooves to dislodge the metal pulp.

ACID SHARPENING

If the file teeth are not too worn, they can be sharpened somewhat by immersing the files in a bath of acid. The acid seems to bite into the walls of the tooth serration, rather than into its edge, and thus sharpens that edge to some degree.

I have successfully used the acid from old car batteries for this purpose. The proprietor of the nearest scrap yard handles turned-in batteries, which he sells for the worth of the lead cells in them and not for the acid. I bring along an acid-proof container and he is glad to let me have all the acid I may need to recondition my files.

To hold the files, use an acid-proof tray such as those used in photographic darkrooms. Carefully pour the battery acid into it. Immerse the files, leaving them in the bath for twelve to twenty-four hours. At once you will see little gas bubbles rising from the files; this indicates that the etching of the steel is taking place. When you think the steel has been etched back enough, fish out one of the files with a pair of pliers, taking care that no acid drippings fall on skin or clothes. Rinse it in running water for a few minutes and dry it. Put a handle on it and try it out on a piece of steel.

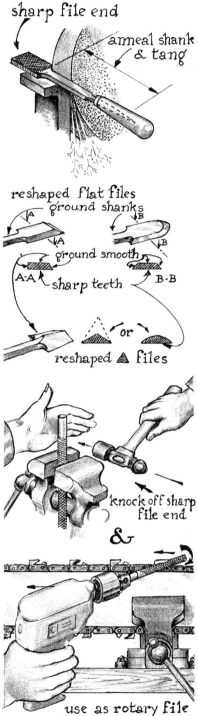

reshaping dull files by grinding on large coarse & hard motor-driven wheels

sharp file end

anneal shank & tang

reshaped flat files
ground shanks
A   B
A   B
ground smooth
A·A   sharp teeth   B·B

or

reshaped ▲ files

knock off sharp file end

&

use as rotary file in chuck of electric drill to sharpen chain saws that are clamped in a vise

If you are satisfied with the sharpness, rinse all the files for long enough to leach out the last trace of acid (an hour or more). The principle is the same as the rinsing of photoprints to leach out the last trace of hypo so that no aftereffect of the chemical will spoil the prints in the future. Any rust discoloration that shows on the files later will not affect their use.

Over the years I have restored dull files in this way at no cost except the time spent.

NOTE: Etching metal with acid need not be dangerous if safety precautions are taken. The main thing to keep in mind is never to handle the liquid with bare skin or breathe the fumes carelessly.

Keep your eyes well protected against splattering from files as they are slid in the acid bath. Also, be aware that the gas emitted by the bubbles is more or less explosive if lighted by flame.

If you have no photographic tray, plastic basins used for household purposes are, as a rule, acid-proof. You can also make a tray from plywood. Coat the wood with beeswax or candlewax, heated over a flame, to make it leak- and acid-proof.

HOW TO KEEP FILES UNCLOGGED

Strange to say, the file's worst enemy, oil or grease, will also keep it unclogged if a minimum coating is used on the serration walls only, not on the sharp edges. A lightly oiled file may not bite into the steel for the first few strokes, but if you bear down hard, and the steel filed upon is soft mild steel, the file *edges* will soon be scraped free of the lubricant and will bite into the steel better than before, at the same time rejecting all filing pulp.

Another approach is to rub into the file from time to time a *chalk powder*, which prevents the metal pulp from getting lodged in the serration grooves.

A file that accidentally gets oily in the shop will not be ruined, as uninformed people claim. Remove the excess oil with a solvent and bear down hard on the file while cutting on mild steel. A dozen strokes or so will restore it if the teeth were sharp to begin with. More than once I have received as a gift such a supposedly "ruined" file. I would have felt almost guilty about accepting it were it not for the fact that the giver insisted positively that it was no longer usable.

RESHAPING OLD WORN FILES

This can be done on a power grinder, but it carries with it the danger of overheating, which will quickly ruin the temper of the steel. Grinding, therefore, must be done very carefully, with frequent cooling of the steel. The illustrations show how to do it.

ROUND FILES

The round files used to resharpen chain saws are discarded when their middle sections have become too dull. Their end sections, which are not used, remain sharp. These can be used as rotary files when clamped in the chuck of a small hand-held electric drill. In this way, chain saws can be sharpened in a fraction of the time that hand-filing would take. A brand-new chain saw file could conceivably be broken up into small rotary file sections to get still more use out of one new file.

When. many years ago, I showed my method to a friend who made his living at cutting wood, his gratitude was unbounded: doing it my way eliminated a major part of his chores.

GRINDING WHEELS

The surfaces of grinding wheels cut in the same way as files do. When using soft, fine-grit wheels that go very slowly, you must oil-saturate them to prevent the metal pulp from clogging the stone's pores. Do it the same way as you would when sharpening tools by hand. Saturate with thin oil and wipe off the metal pulp from time to time before adding more oil.

If a wheel rotates fast, the centrifugal force will throw off excess oil. After that use a toothed steel dressing wheel to sharpen the cutting surface somewhat. You will find that an oil-treated wheel grinds the softer metals with much less tendency to clogging than an unoiled one does.

Should mild or high-carbon steel be ground on very coarse, hard, dry wheels running at 1700 rpm or more, no lubrication against clogging is needed since the metal pulp will be thrown off by centrifugal force.

MAKING FILES AND RASPS

It is not difficult to make a fairly crude file, but handmade files cannot compete with machine-made industrial ones. In any critical filing job, machine-made files should be used. If, however, you are in emergency need of a particular file and the nearest supply house is too far away, you can make one without too much difficulty.

Forge the file blank from high-carbon steel stock. Anneal it slowly to its softest. Fasten the blank on an end-grain piece of wood clamped in the vise.

Any sharp-edged cold chisel, held in a fairly upright position and struck with a heavy hammer, can raise a sharp cutting edge like those of a file. The illustrations give an idea of what happens when the angles at which the bevels of cold chisels are ground cut the steel in various ways. They can form fine or blunt teeth depending on the slant of the chisel to the surface of the file blank.

It is true that any sharp, raised part of a piece of steel will, when hardened correctly, cut steel like a file. But centuries of experience in file-making have taught manufacturers which angle and which combination of spacing and cross-cutting of the teeth will give the best results. These findings have been applied in designing file-making machines that cut file teeth at their most effective and uniform. Readers will find that hand-cut file teeth can produce a usable file even though it may be less refined than machine-cut files.

use cold chisel edge to cut steel surfaces or raise file & rasp teeth

steel surface is cut in a hacking action

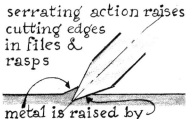

serrating action raises cutting edges in files & rasps

metal is raised by wedge action

bastard file teeth are cut deep & spaced farther apart smooth files are cut shallow & more finely serrated

raised spaced &

bastard files are more

smooth files are less spaced & raised

chisel direction raises teeth in a wedge action

15°

chisel facet keeps groove bottom open

wedge forces

for best results:
space between teeth equal
depth of teeth equal
each hammer blow to 1 tooth
all blows of the same force
groove bottoms somewhat rounded

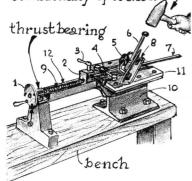

file-making rig made from waste materials & manually operated

thrust bearing

1 disc settings measure spacing between file teeth
2-3 clamps file stock 7 which is moved by threaded rod 9
4-5 rubber rollers press file stock & chisel 6 in their tracks
8 frame holds 6-5 & is bolted onto 10
10 is I beam section onto which are riveted bridge-plates 11

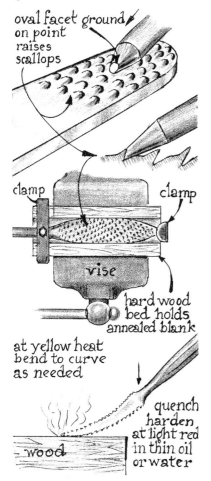

oval facet ground on point raises scallops

clamp   clamp

vise

hard wood bed holds annealed blank

at yellow heat bend to curve as needed

wood

quench harden at light red in thin oil or water

A File-Cutting Jig

You can put together a file-cutting jig in your home shop if you wish to spend the time.

Examine the illustrated detail of an enlarged file tooth. Analyze what takes place. A cold chisel can be used to raise a sharp edge on the file blank a few hundred times. If the teeth are as evenly spaced as possible and uniformly struck by hand, a moderately useful file will result. Only correct hardening is needed to finish the job.

A File Made from Mild Steel

File teeth can be cut in a short time without danger of dulling the cold chisel. Once all teeth are cut, heat the whole piece evenly to *yellow heat* and sprinkle case-hardening compound over the toothed surface of the file.

When the workpiece is replaced in the forge fire, the hardening compound will bubble and melt until all of it has been consumed. At that moment, brittle quench the file in brine or water. Since the teeth edges are very thin, the hardening effect of the powder easily penetrates all the way.

It is remarkable how well such a tool will stand up in an emergency, and the same can be said for a case-hardened mild steel rasp.

Making Rasps

Instead of a cold chisel, a pointed tool is used to form the teeth. The cutting point is created by grinding a small slanted oval facet on the end of a one-point stone-carving tool. Hold the tool at a slant to the prepared surface of the rasp blank and strike it with a one-pound hammer. A single tooth is thus bent outward from the surface.

The next tooth can be placed as you choose. The illustration shows a pattern with staggered teeth. With practice, you will be able to cut teeth as regular as those seen in skillfully handmade Italian rasps. It is an inspiration for a naturally dexterous person to learn how to make good rasps by hand.

NOTE: Files and rasps made of high-carbon tool steel should be heated a *light cherry red* and quenched in thin oil or brine. This gives the teeth a hardness to cut mild steel or annealed high-carbon steel. At the same time the softer core of the file makes it resistant to breaking under strain.

If a piece from the scrap pile proves to be barely temperable, you may have to heat it a little *lighter* than light cherry red in order to obtain the hardness needed. Quenching in water will then be most effective. Be careful, however, that the visible heat glow stops where the tool's tang begins so that the tang will not break off at the handle after quenching.

Rotary Files and Rasps

Blanks made for rotary files and rasps can first be turned on a lathe. The profile can be cylindrical or any shape you like. The shanks are finished to fit the chuck of a small hand-held electric drill or a table-mounted arbor.

Place its working part in a bed carved into the end-grain surface of a block of wood. (Pear, maple, or a comparable fine-grained wood is preferable.) Cut teeth serrations into its upper exposed surface, as in a file, or individual scalloped teeth, as in a rasp.

After all the teeth have been cut in the exposed surface, lift the blank out of its bed and turn it over, seating it with the textured surface on the wood below. In this way the raised teeth will not be damaged during the cutting of the rest of the teeth.

After the rotary files and rasps have been hardened, it is wise to use a propane torch to locally anneal their tang stems with a pinpoint flame. A protective shield made of asbestos or metal can be slipped over the teeth to keep the flame away from the working end.

Making a Cylindrical Rotary Rasp

Although high-carbon steel is preferred for rotary rasps, they can also be made from a section of plumbing pipe or fitting. When using plumbing material, grind off the outside galvanization or cut it off on the lathe. This eliminates any interference with later case-hardening treatment.

Cut a 2-inch length from a standard 1-inch galvanized plumbing pipe. Next turn from a well-seasoned piece of hardwood a core that fits tightly within the pipe and clamp the assembly in the lathe chuck.

With a 3/8-inch diameter drill in the tailstock chuck, drill a hole through the core to receive an arbor. When the two have been assembled, clamp the arbor in the lathe chuck. The outside of the galvanized tube can now be turned to clean off every trace of the galvanized outer skin while aligning the piece as well. The unit is now ready to be held in a hardwood bed where the teeth can be cut and, finally, case hardened.

There is no limit to the number and variety of files and rasps that can be made once the craftsman has seen how quick and simple it is to make them in his own shop, from scrap material. The skill is useful when odd shaped tools that cannot be bought in stores are required to fit specific needs.

20. The Reverse Lathe

stationary lathe drives the workpiece

headstock center drives

hand-held tool moves to cut

However

when process is reversed a movable lathe is hand held & guided to effect cutting on contact with rotary cutter

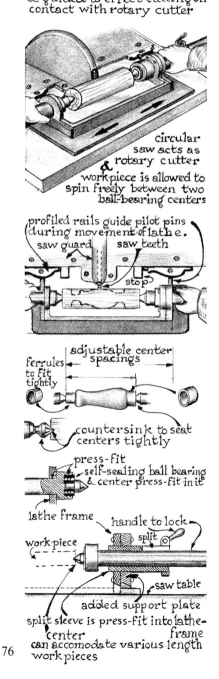

circular saw acts as a rotary cutter

workpiece is allowed to spin freely between two ball-bearing centers

profiled rails guide pilot pins during movement of lathe.

saw guard   saw teeth

stop

adjustable center spacings

ferrules to fit tightly

countersink to seat centers tightly

press-fit self-sealing ball bearing & center press-fit in it

lathe frame   handle to lock

workpiece   split

saw table

added support plate

split sleeve is press-fit into lathe-frame

center can accomodate various length workpieces

The reverse lathe is the opposite of the conventional lathe, which has a headstock that drives the workpiece while the hand-held cutting tool, placed on a steady rest, cuts the driven workpiece. In a reverse lathe, a small movable lathe is hand held and guides the workpiece against a driven cutter. On contact, the workpiece is spun and cut at the same time.

The illustrations make clear the advantages of the setup. Instead of using a circular saw, any kind of stationary rotary cutter would be suitable.

Such a reverse lathe must have two adjustable tail centers to allow a workpiece to spin freely when it is brought into contact with the driven cutter element. The workpiece will start to spin instantly, but its inertia will cause the speed to be slightly less than the speed of the moving cutter teeth or blades; that is why a cutting action takes place. By moving the workpiece back and forth in front of the cutter, you will be able to shear off the wood that is in the way of the cutter.

The illustrated example shows stationary profile rails along which pilot pins slide to direct the movement of the reverse lathe assembly. After repeated back-and-forth movements have cut all material in the cutter's path, these pilot pins contact the profile rail at every point, showing that the job has been completed.

The whole operation, from start to finish, can be done in a few seconds for such simple projects as wood handles for carving tools, files, and other hand-held tools.

To refine the wood surface, transfer the reverse lathe and its workpiece to a stationary rotating sanding disc with a rubber backing. The spinning workpiece, in contact with the rotating sanding disc, can be smoothed in a few seconds.

Any further refining of wood surfaces can then be done first with shellac fillers and then with waxed cotton buffers. Being able to hand-manipulate the reverse lathe assembly against any sander or buffer so easily makes the setup very practical.

APPLICATIONS FOR THE REVERSE LATHE

The illustrations show an application of the reverse lathe principle: how to grind engine valves in a fraction of the time that it would take on more complex grinding machinery.

With a machinist-blacksmith shop, it is fairly simple to make both instruments. I have done this with results that could not be improved upon. It must be remembered, however, that, as with all material presented in this book, each craftsman who aims to make things from scrap material will come up with an instrument that looks different, but which works in the same way as the ones shown here.

EXTENDED USE OF THE REVERSE LATHE

Once you have tried out the reverse lathe, you will be able to visualize many other applications that use a variety of cutting elements. When the forms of the workpieces have been established roughly, the surfaces can be refined with stationary anchored rotary files, rasps, grindstones, or rubber-backed flexible sanding discs. Sand-blasting tips can also act as combination drivers and cutters.

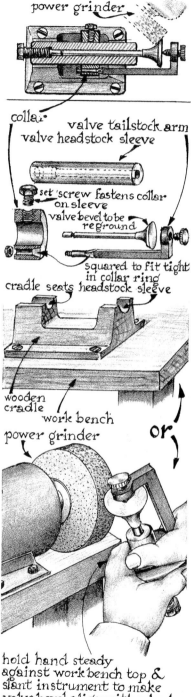

engine valve grinding-jig is hand held in wooden cradle which is fastened to workbench

power grinder

collar

valve tailstock arm
valve headstock sleeve

set screw fastens collar on sleeve

valve bevel to be reground

squared to fit tight in collar ring
cradle seats headstock sleeve

wooden cradle

work bench

power grinder

or

hold hand steady against work bench top & slant instrument to make valve-bevel align with wheel surface under an angle which causes a slow valve-spin during grinding **next**

refine surface texture on a fine grit side-grinder

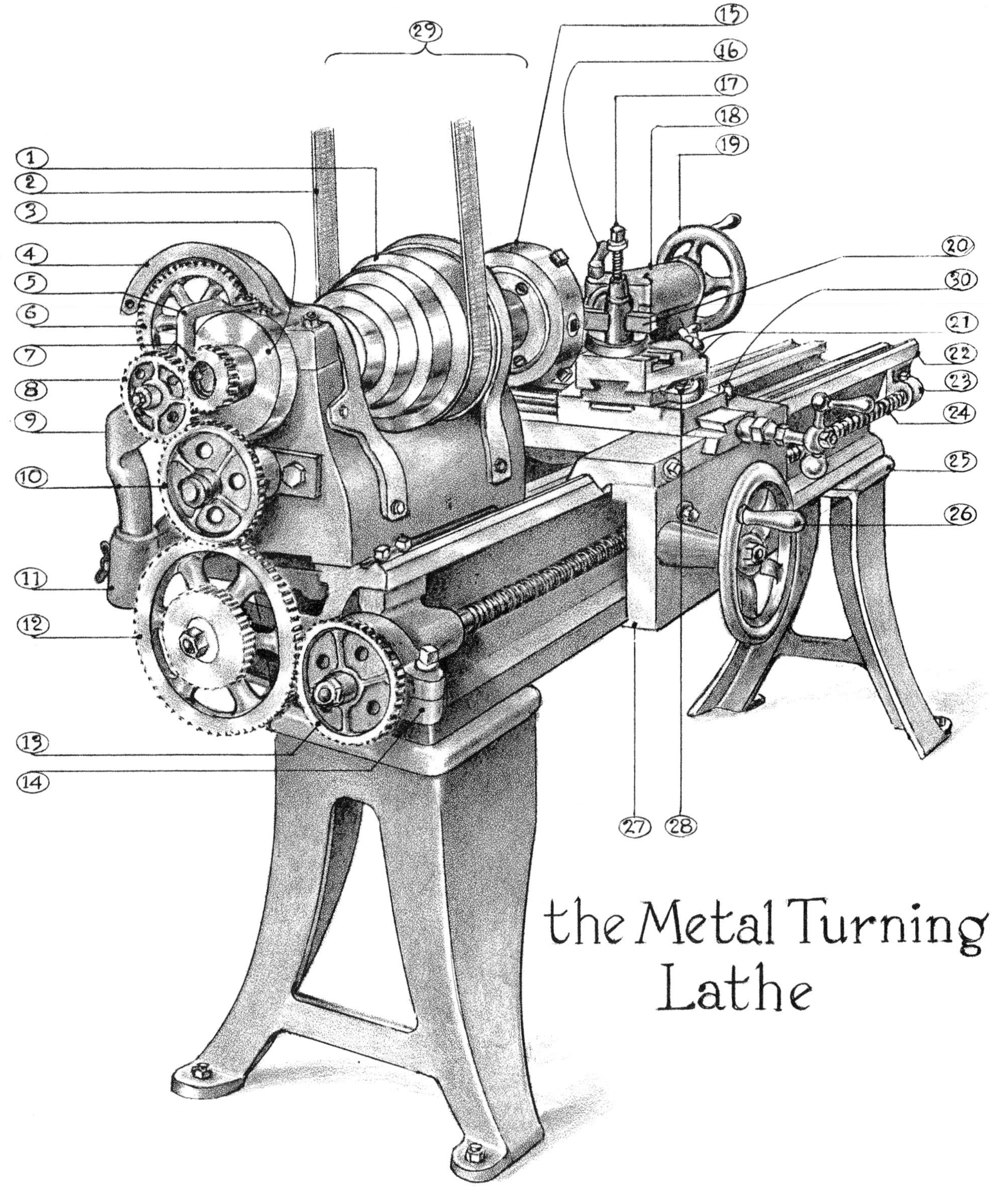

the Metal Turning Lathe

1 headstock step pulley
2 drive belt
3 main ballbearing
4 backgear guard
5 top part of unit 9
6 back gear
7 main drive pinion gear
8 intermediate gear
9 bracket holding 8
10 intermediate gear
11 bracket socket

12 interchange gear
13 interchange gear
14 adjustable frame for 12 & 13
15 head stock chuck
16 tailstock locking handle
17 tool post locking screw
18 tailstock
19 tailstock feeding wheel
20 tool bit holder
21 tool post bed & tool feed handle
22 lathe bed

23 lead screw bearing
24 leadscrew spindle
25 carriage cross feed handle
26 handle for longitudinal feed
27 carriage unit
28 angle positioning lock screw
29 head stock assembly
30 carriage locking screw

not shown: automatic cross-feed & longitudinal feed units

21. How to Recycle and Operate a Metal-Turning Lathe

In the year 1880 in Holland, my father was taught how to operate a machinist's lathe as part of his training to become a marine engineer in the East Indies navy.

The difference between his training and mine, in Holland in 1915 to 1923, made me realize that the lathe had come a long way since the hand-held cutting tools used for turning metal in his time. By my time, they had been completely eliminated.

The lathe that I used in technical school in 1919, though old and worn, seemed a fine piece of machinery. Overhead transmission shafts connected all shop machines with idling and live pulley units from which a belt reached a machine tool below it. The machine tools were driven by a one-cylinder, 25 hp, large bore horizontal steam engine with a huge flywheel.

Standing at the lathe one could easily reach overhead to a wooden handle ending in a fork with which to move the belt from the idler to the live pulley, thus engaging the lathe. Once connected, it took a split second before the back-geared lathe headstock would move. This was because wear and tear had created so much play in the machine parts that in back gearing it took a moment for the slack to be taken up. But once the headstock was moving in the well-oiled and accurate sleeve bearings, remarkably precise work could be done on the old lathe.

Visualize, then, a lathe of that vintage to be found in many home shops today. They are still being sold by families whose fathers and grandfathers ran independent shops or used such a lathe to pursue their hobbies in retirement years.

With the nationwide revival of handcrafts today, many modern craftsmen enhance their shops with these old machine tools. Once dusted off, cleaned, oiled, and renovated, the old, sturdy metal-turning lathe will serve its present owner extremely well as a recycled machine tool.

I myself came by such a lathe, and a few weeks of repair work on it enabled me to do all the lathe work needed in my shop, where I combine blacksmithing and machinist-type activities. My experiences may help you learn how to recycle and use old, worn machine tools so that you can get by with what you have.

My lathe is a 1919 South Bend all-purpose model. The bed measures 6 feet in length and I can cut a 15-inch circle. Missing were all the gears for thread-cutting as well as the one gear that linked the headstock pinion gear with the gear that drives the tool carriage longitudinal lead screw to make automatic feed possible. It had a three-jaw self-centering chuck, but was missing a four-jaw chuck, a faceplate, and a lathe dog. I easily forged the lathe dog and turned an adaptable faceplate to be clamped in the three-jaw chuck.

As luck would have it, a friend had given me, twenty years before, a box of small gears that had belonged to a smaller lathe of unknown

recycling an old metal-turning lathe

forged bracket **A** takes stub-shaft **B** to anchor the transmission gear **b**

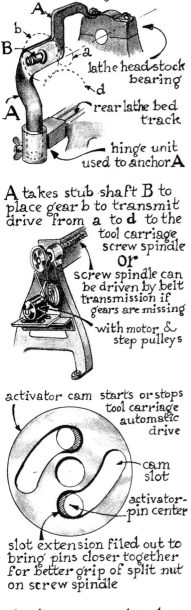

lathe headstock bearing

rear lathe bed track

hinge unit used to anchor **A**

A takes stub shaft **B** to place gear **b** to transmit drive from **a** to **d** to the tool carriage screw spindle

or

screw spindle can be driven by belt transmission if gears are missing

with motor & step pulleys

activator cam starts or stops tool carriage automatic drive

cam slot

activator-pin center

slot extension filed out to bring pins closer together for better grip of split nut on screw spindle

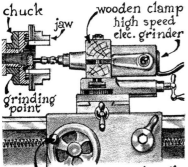

chuck

jaw

wooden clamp

high speed elec. grinder

grinding point

tool carriage activator handle

vintage. Lo and behold, it turned out that the pitch of the teeth on these narrower gears was the same as on the wider ones of my old lathe! All I had to do was to turn adapter sleeves to make up for the difference in shaft diameters. Once the keys, dowels, and idling sleeves were installed, almost any lathe work could be handled very well, with one exception: the cutting of all the different threads. I had to juggle my narrower little gears around to do this, which would take quite some time.

But in practice I found myself more often cutting thread by placing a tap in the headstock and, with the lathe in back gearing, pushing the workpiece into alignment against it with the tailstock center feeding-screw.

In a similar way, one can easily cut a thread on bars clamped tightly in the headstock using one of the many threading dies one seems to accumulate over the years. Keep the die from moving by clamping a visegrip plier on the housing handle and push the die forward with a suitable adapter placed in the tailstock. Let the visegrip or die-housing handle follow by sliding over the tool post bed.

The major gain these narrow compromise gears gave me was to permit the tool carriage to move automatically again. For this I had to forge a complicated bracket in order to bolt to it a steel stub shaft. This shaft holds a transmission gear that connects the headstock pinion gear with a large idling gear, which in turn moves the lead screw spindle in the carriage. Thus I can cut long pieces of work automatically and evenly.

The need for an automatic carriage drive must have been felt by the previous owner of this machine tool. Not having the gears, he had installed on a bracket bolted to the lathe leg a quarter-horse electric motor. With a step pulley on the motor and one on the lathe lead screw, he could vary the moving speed of the tool carriage at will, thus bypassing a gear drive he did not have.

This points up the fact that, if worse comes to worse, belt-driven transmission arrangements will do well in a home shop. Do not hesitate to be inventive in these matters. There is a choice of the widest variety among the many kinds of transmission systems in salvaged machinery, including automobiles. For instance, chain transmissions of timing gears in cars would be ideal, since the parts can be exposed and center-to-center distances can be made adjustable with an idler roller.

Another worn element in this lathe that had to be reactivated was the split lead screw housing, which engages or disengages the tool carriage's longitudinal feeding movement. This screw housing had worn to the point that it skipped a beat. Taking apart its eccentric coupling, I simply extended its cam slot with a rotary file. That allowed the housing activators to move a bit further so that the split lead screw housing could clamp onto the screw a little more tightly, engaging it effectively. It was the brass screw housing, not the lead screw spindle, that had worn.

Next came the inaccurate three-jaw chuck, which had to be made accurate again. If an accurate round workpiece, free from a tailstock center, is clamped into a three-jaw chuck, its end generally shows a little wobble, especially when the workpiece is a fairly long rod. Often this is a sign that the chuck jaws have worn at one end more than the other. This telltale sign means that regrinding the jaws is called for if, after several tries, it continues to show an end wobble.

GRINDING CHUCK JAWS FOR ACCURACY

As the illustration shows, I made a wooden mount for my electric grinder so that it could be clamped onto the tool post bed. By aligning the grinder unit with the chuck center, I ensured that its grinding point could enter the opening between the chuck jaws and could be made to move freely back and forth between them over their full length.

Rotating the headstock at slow rpm in direct drive, I cross-fed the grinding point gently outward toward me until the first spark showed contact between the point and the steel of the chuck jaw. Next, moving the lathe carriage back and forth evenly by hand, I brought the grinding point into contact with the full length of each of the jaws. From time to time I would increase the bite of the grinding point by 1/1000 of an inch. I could tell upon examination if all three jaws had been resurfaced by the grinding points, thus correcting them. Any further grinding was unnecessary; it would only reduce the lifetime of the jaws.

Wear and tear in the chuck body itself must also be met. It would show up after forceful tightening of the chuck jaws onto an accurately round workpiece. If the jaws grab the workpiece at the jaw base ends and not at the jaw tip ends, it will produce some wobble at the free end of the workpiece. To compensate for such chuck wear, the grinding must be graduated from jaw tip to jaw base in order to space the jaw base ends 1/1000 or 2/1000 of an inch farther outward than the tips. This makes it possible for all jaws to be clamped on the workpiece over their full length with even bearing instead of on one end only.

Another improvement for an old, worn, three-jaw chuck that can no longer clamp very small diameter work is as follows:

Remove the jaws, but first make certain that each jaw is marked with a stamped-in number or code corresponding to the proper location on the chuck body. This assures correct replacement, and most chucks do have such matching marks stamped in.

Regrinding each chuck jaw as shown in the illustration reduces the width of the contact area with the workpiece so that all three jaws can come centrally closer together. Since each jaw has been hardened to hold fast to mild steel workpieces, it is the workpiece that will wear down under jaw slippage. But if the piece should be *harder* than the jaws, such slippage will wear down the jaws.

I suggest that the contact groove width between jaws and workpiece not be smaller than 3/16 inch for a lathe of a 12-inch workpiece diameter or over.

CLAMPING OUT-OF-ROUND OR ECCENTRIC WORKPIECES IN THREE-JAW CHUCKS

It is necessary to position such a piece by using a filler shim or strip between one of the jaws and the workpiece. The filler strip should be the length of the jaw itself so that at no point can an uneven clamping action take place. A simple probe between tool post and rotating workpiece will easily show if the piece has been centered correctly, where such centering is required. (In industry a finely sensitive dial indicator probe is used to measure off-center movements.)

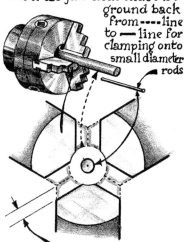

repairing parts of a worn metal-turning lathe

worn 120° jaw ends must be ground back from ---- line to — line for clamping onto small diameter rods

120° facets ground back

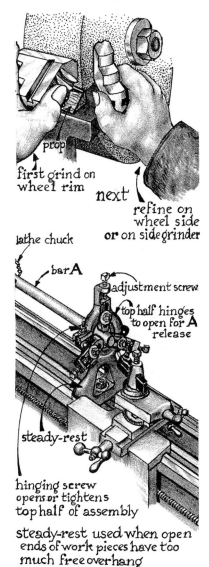

first grind on wheel rim

next

refine on wheel side or on side grinder

lathe chuck

bar A

adjustment screw

top half hinges to open for A release

steady-rest

hinging screw opens or tightens top half of assembly

steady-rest used when open ends of work pieces have too much free overhang

TURNING OPEN-ENDED WORKPIECES

This means that no tailstock is used when turning a long piece that is clamped in the three-jaw chuck. First place the tool bit elevation position at dead center so that no workpiece center remnant will force the tool bit below it during rotation. Otherwise great strains might pull the workpiece out of center in the chuck or break the tool bit at its point. There is a real danger when using carbon-tipped tools that such brittle bits will then break.

Another make-ready method is to center-punch the bar ending and position it onto the tailstock center before tightening its other end in the headstock chuck.

The Lathe Steady-rest

If the free end of a long bar must be faced or bored or shaped, a steady-rest can be placed at its end.

Clamp the bar in the chuck and test run it without the steady-rest. If the end of the workpiece shows no significant wobble, position the steady-rest assembly, as shown, for a cutting action to come.

In this aligned position, with the workpiece at rest, hand screw the loosened steadying sliding sleeves, one after the other, onto the bar end until each gently touches its surface. Next oil the contact area between sleeve ends and workpiece and run the headstock in direct drive. Now move each sleeve inward somewhat with the wrench and temporarily secure each one at the moment that a little dragging of the workpiece surface between the sleeves takes place. At this point, minutely retract the sleeves just enough to stop the dragging, then tighten them in their slots to anchor them securely. In this way all elements seek their own best positions without binding after being locked in place.

You may now begin cutting without worrying about the workpiece moving out of center, its outward face freely exposed to the cutting tip.

TOOL BIT SHARPENING

The beginner, taking his first steps in working at the machinist's lathe, must soon learn the design principles of shaping and sharpening tool bits.

Tool bit profiles must slant *away* from the workpiece to make them bite into the steel effectively. The illustrations show what is involved. Professional lathe operators offer much advice on how to angle the tool bits to make them cut at their best, and there is no doubt that experimentation and scientific analysis have established the exact profile angle for lathe cutting bits for every imaginable set of circumstances. They must be tailored to cut workpieces of different diameters, hardness, types of metal, etc. For all-around purposes, however, and especially in the shop geared to a one-man operation, one soon learns to "feel" how a cutting bit should be shaped and sharpened once one understands what takes place when metal is cut. I have found that such an empirical approach gives me excellent results in most situations.

It is very important to keep in mind that the grinding angles should not weaken the bit unnecessarily. They should *just clear* the workpiece below the actual cutting edge to avoid binding or dragging. A

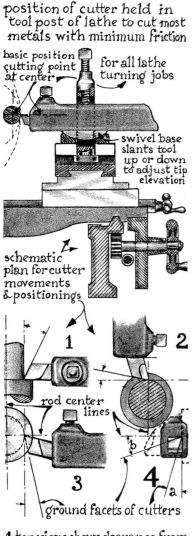

position of cutter held in tool post of lathe to cut most metals with minimum friction

basic position cutting point at center — for all lathe turning jobs

swivel base slants tool up or down to adjust tip elevation

schematic plan for cutter movements & positionings

rod center lines

ground facets of cutters

1 top view shows clearance from longitudinal straight rod if cutter tip at height of rod center

2 & 3 clearance from vertical tangent plane to rod circle

4 angle a' clears cutting tip from binding against side faces, & angle b helps the cut metal to ease off the tip unbroken

cutting bit should be positioned in such a way that the steel will not only be cut easily, but that the track it leaves on the steel surface becomes almost polished at the same time. It is good practice, if the cutting bit seems to cut properly, to lubricate it as well to insure smoothness of operation and to keep workpieces and cutters cool. There are many of us who do not care to purchase special lubrication liquids for lathe operation. Used motor oil will do; a small stiff brush in a can of oil kept within arm's reach serves very well.

DIFFERENCES BETWEEN CUTTING TOOLS FOR WOOD-TURNING AND METAL-TURNING

Because wood is softer than steel, wood-turning tools can have thin, sharp-angled edges. But tools for cutting steel must have edges that are thicker and blunt-angled. The thicker edges for steel cutting, therefore, do not slope away from the workpiece as much as do the edges of wood-cutting tools. (See Chapter 6, page 28.)

I suggest that, when tailoring lathe tool cutting edges, the beginner not hesitate to experiment, even at the expense of a few misjudgments. He can gain from mistakes and thereby learn to do the right thing at the right time.

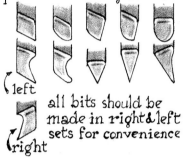

most often used cutting bit profiles for turning metals

(left

all bits should be made in right & left sets for convenience

(right

THE HEADSTOCK FACEPLATE AND THE LATHE DOG

If no faceplate is available you can duplicate its action by holding the workpiece between two lathe center points. First turn a center with a cylindrical shank and clamp it in the three-jaw chuck; clamp a lathe dog onto the workpiece. Such a dog can be forged so that its arm will reach between the chuck jaw's walls, thus driving the workpiece with it. This duplicates the faceplate-lathe dog setup.

Advantages of Using the Lathe Dog Method

The greatest value in this method is that the tailstock body can be adjusted horizontally under right angles with the lathe bed, creating an offset between centers of headstock and tailstock. Such an offset makes it possible to cut a cylindrical workpiece into a tapered one with the cutter travelling parallel to the lathe bed. Another advantage is that inaccuracies of the chuck can be completely ignored as long as the center inset clamped in the chuck is made to move in true center.

This center, as well as the one in the tailstock, acts in reality like a universal joint to the workpiece center seatings, driving it in perfectly centralized rotation free from any possible chuck-induced tensions. See to it that the head- and tailstock centers are kept well lubricated. An additional advantage of this method is that the workpiece can easily be removed from the lathe whenever needed and replaced between centers again without risking any variation in the positioning of the workpiece.

HOW TO CUT A TAPER

If we wish to make a duplicate tailstock center shank with a Morse taper we can do so without any measuring instruments at all, using sighting methods only.

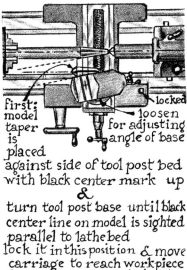

cutting tapers on a lathe
1ˢᵗ method

first: model taper is placed against side of tool post bed with black center mark up
&
turn tool post base until black center line on model is sighted parallel to lathe bed
lock it in this position & move carriage to reach workpiece for cutting action & lock it too.
feed cutter with tool bed screw, only

locked
loosen for adjusting angle of base

First Method

Keep the tailstock center aligned to the headstock center. The tool post body, being adjustable, can be rotated horizontally to any angle you wish and locked at that new angle. Feeding the cutter with the tool post body only will then cut the workpiece at that new angle while the lathe carriage is securely locked to the lathe bed. The Morse taper, however, happens to be measured, not in degrees, but by offset and distance—in this case 5/8 inch to the foot. The measure is an approximation because Mr. Morse, the inventor of this tool's design, found that the required taper angles had to differ a bit when these center inserts were used to hold fast to large or small diameter workpieces. The design of the center's taper shank is intended to give it a holding capacity, as a clutch does, without freezing into its seat and making it difficult to extract.

Using your own center inset as a model, place it on a blackened, flat, machined surface so that a black line rubs off on the inset. This mark will enable you to hold the inset tangentially against the side of the adjustable tool post assembly with the horizontal black line facing vertically upward. Rotate the loosened tool post assembly while sighting as accurately as possible until the black line runs parallel to the lathe bed below. At that angle, lock the tool post bed position.

You can now begin cutting at the start of the cutter's travel span and the beginning of the tail-center end of the workpiece. After several cuts have brought the workpiece to a size that can be tested for a fit of its taper angle in the tailstock center sleeve, stop the lathe, slide back the tailstock assembly, and remove the center from the tailstock.

Next, remove the center's sleeve and slip it over the as yet unfinished lathe-turned end that remains in the chuck. If you find that only the smallest or largest diameter of the partially turned taper shank contacts the sleeve, it means that the angle adjustment of the tool post assembly must be corrected. This time, you could hold the model tangentially against the workpiece in a reverse directed taper position. Its center black marking line should run parallel to the lathe bed. If it doesn't, the tool post bed position should be corrected accordingly.

Still another way is to estimate the amount of play by rocking the sleeve at deepest insert of the unfinished taper shank and to adjust the angle setting by feel.

After adjustment, make a new cut, which, as a rule, will prove to be so nearly accurate that only the tiniest adjustment, if any, is needed. Tapping sideways with a small hammer or mallet on the end of the slightly loosened tool post body will reposition the tool post bed almost imperceptibly. If the test (sleeve over taper) shows the angle to be correct, proceed to duplicate the model for size and length, after which the sleeve should show a perfect seating when placed over the new taper.

NOTE: In most lathes of this nature the limited tool travel requires more than one full run. To reach the final taper shank length the lathe carriage must be loosened, moved up a little, locked on the lathe bed once more, and the cutting continued where it was left off.

After the final test, refine the taper shank's texture further if needed with a fine-grit, rubber-backed abrasive disc held in a small electric drill rotating against the surface of the taper as it rotates in the headstock. When the surface texture shows even and smooth, cut off the needed part of the workpiece. This is the blank out of which the head of the tailstock center piece can be turned to meet the design planned for it.

Second Method

This method uses the faceplate and dog. A suitable size rod (not longer than necessary) is first provided with deep drilled center seatings at both ends so that it can be held snugly between headstock and tailstock centers. Again, the surface of the model center inset is marked with a black line. With that horizontal line facing upward, hold the model horizontally and tangentially against the rod (workpiece stock).

Next, turn the adjusting screws on the tailstock base to an offset position until you sight the black line on the model as parallel to the lathe bed below it. In this way, you can determine the tailstock center position. Secure it in that position.

Begin the cutting with a shallow cut. Feed it with the lathe carriage back and forth along the rotating dog-driven rod. As soon as enough of the length of the taper has been turned for an angle test, remove the workpiece and slip it into the emptied tailstock sleeve. If necessary, adjust the position of the tailstock setting with the two offset screws to meet whatever inaccuracy you have observed, and restore the setup for the next cut. After that cut has been made, test it again and continue this procedure until a perfect fit has been established.

When the taper is finished, return the tailstock center to lathe center with the tailstock offset adjusting screws.

Whatever type head you wish to turn on a new blank for a tailstock center can now be done in the normal way.

HOW TO MARK THE TOOL POST BODY ON THE TOOL POST BED FOR A MORSE TAPER ANGLE

On the end of a flat-ended punch, grind a right angle cutting edge. Place it at a chosen spot and match the right angles between tool post body and tool post bed. Strike a light but telling blow on the punch. This leaves the two meeting lines indented in the upright and horizontal metal parts, indicating the correct position of the tool post body for cutting a Morse taper. It allows instant and accurate positioning of the tool post assembly for future occasions. No such mark can be made on the tailstock body since the needed offset differs with the length of the workpiece held between lathe centers.

NOTE: Trial and error methods in lathe-turning versus sophisticated industry methods have been adequate when making tools out of worn and discarded machines and parts. Instead of using refined measuring instruments, I would need occasionally a regular inside and outside caliper, a depth gauge, and such ordinary tools as a square, a straight edge, a pair of dividers.

HARDENING TAIL-CENTER TIPS

Since the central seatings of workpieces turn around tail-center tips in the same way that shafts and bearings rotate around one another, the center tip surface must be hard, polished, and lubricated in order to stand up under the great strains and friction created by heavy cuts made with the tool bit.

Harden the tips by drawing a *straw color* after brittle quenching. Be cautioned that the tip must be heated *very slowly* in the forge until that tip begins to glow locally to a *light cherry red*. At that time the slow heating has spread the heat gradually, through the steel's con-

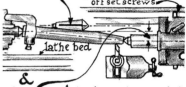

2ⁿᵈ method

place model taper with center black mark up to work piece
off set screws
lathe bed

&
offset tailstock center until black line is sighted parallel to lathe bed
next: position carriage & tool post assembly for cutting action & feeding tool parallel to lathe bed with either one

marking punch
90°

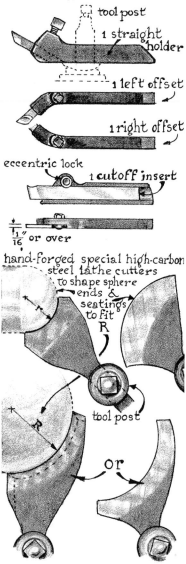

holders for high speed steel cutter-bits

tool post

1 straight holder

1 left offset

1 right offset

eccentric lock

1 cutoff insert

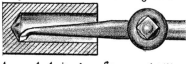

$\frac{1}{16}$" or over

hand-forged special high-carbon steel lathe cutters to shape sphere ends & seatings to fit

R

tool post

or

high-carbon steel boring tool

bores hole to size after pre-drilling with shop forged & ground drill fed by lathe tailstock & held from turning with visegrip pliers.

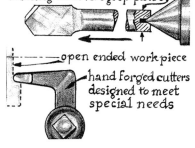

open ended workpiece

hand forged cutters designed to meet special needs

ductivity, while not heating up the shank part of the taper to a critical degree. A sudden quench will, therefore, keep that shank fairly soft, which will give it a better holding ability than a hardened, highly polished shank would. After all, taper and sleeve act more or less as a clutch does to keep its opposite member from slipping while letting it go easily when necessary.

STANDARD AND SPECIAL METAL-TURNING LATHE CUTTING TOOLS

Almost all metal-turning lathes are provided with an adjustable tool post. The slot in the tool post can hold the standard lathe cutting-tip holders. It is advisable to have in one's collection a straight holder, and a lefthanded and righthanded one. A holder that can contain a cut-off blade insert is recommended. The same tool post can hold handmade cutters forged from high-carbon tool steel and ground to suit. In this instance the correct dimensions of a sphere, or a seating in which such a sphere might fit, can be used to make cup shapes as shown in Chapter 26. The preliminary shaping of such spheres and sphere seatings with standard lathe cutting tools can be followed up with the special tools for a last refined cut.

These special tools are very convenient and, as a rule, any machinist who is a blacksmith as well can easily and quickly make all lathe cutters from scrap steel. Boring tools for small hole diameters are especially easy and quick to forge. That goes for the forging of any size drill as well. If a workpiece can be clamped in the headstock chuck and such a drill fed with the tailstock center at slow rpm, drilling large holes becomes a simple matter.

Another tool, the right-angle cutter, designed to cut open-faced projects on the lathe, is readily forged. It can reach close quarters in complicated setups, simplifying make-readies.

USING THE LATHE IN PREFERENCE TO THE DRILL PRESS

It is difficult to drill holes larger than 1/2 inch in diameter on a standard modern drill press because its slowest speed is often too fast. If you have no means to reduce the speed, the metal-turning lathe is the solution. Everyone who owns a metal-turning lathe should acquire a drill chuck insert with a Morse taper shank that fits the lathe tailstock, or should adapt one by having it welded onto a Morse taper shank.

The drill, placed in the chuck, can thus be fed by the tailstock screw if a workpiece lends itself to being clamped in the headstock chuck. The illustration shows the setup in which the drill is placed just before touching the workpiece. It is cradled in a V-slot ground into the end of a standard lathe cutter-holder. In this position, the slot may be moved sideways without pushing the drill forward. Thus the drill can slide snugly along the slot walls, which keep the drill from wandering once it engages the workpiece. You will quickly learn how to meet the slightest deviation in position of all elements involved in this simple method of securing exact drill alignment with the workpiece rotation.

Sometimes the drill tip must be steadied further in the slot by pushing the drill tip a little more sideways. The cutting edge of the drill tip then acts as a lathe cutter-bit placed in that position until enough of a bite has been made in the workpiece to create a central seating for the drill tip. Gradually backing off the tool-holder guide while feeding the drill with the tailstock will soon establish correct alignment so that the tool-holder guide can be moved out of the way.

This system is especially convenient should you wish to drill very small holes at high speed without having to make a centerpunch mark in the workpiece beforehand. Such small holes are needed before using a very large drill with a leading pin. The leading pin fits into that small hole and is fed into the workpiece at the slowest speed of the lathe in back-gearing. A common difficulty is that drilling large holes will make the drill shank slip in the chuck, which often cannot be tightened sufficiently to prevent it from doing so. In that case, a visegrip plier clamped firmly onto a small, flat facet ground on the drill shank will keep the shank from slipping under such strains.

Instead of a drill chuck, the tailstock center inset can hold the drill. In this setup, the drill shank should have a deep center seating to hold the drill onto the tip of the tailstock center inset. A small, flat facet should be ground onto the shank so that a wrench or visegrip plier can be clamped over it to keep the drill from turning.

CAUTION: There is danger that the drill shank will slip off the tail-stock center tip if the feeding of the drill is slackened during drilling. This could make the drill "grab" the workpiece sideways, thereby breaking it.

It is remarkable how effectively such important drilling jobs can be carried out, especially if one has to bore large holes in workpieces that can be clamped into the headstock chuck. Predrilling of the large hole will simplify a much larger diameter boring job to be done later.

Using the Headstock Chuck to Hold the Drill

This must be done if the workpiece cannot be clamped into the headstock chuck. The illustration shows a setup in which part of the workpiece rests on the top of the tool post assembly to slide along it during drilling. In this instance, the tailstock center is shown re-moved and the sleeve pushes against a wooden block, which allows the hole to be drilled all the way through instead of partway.

It is easy to see that endless combinations of drilling problems can be solved using a lathe with different setups. The main thing is to stay within the range of possibilities that the tools offer and not to overreach ourselves to the point that we break tools needlessly. Many tools are broken and ruined by overloading or speeding.

USING THE LATHE AS A MILLING MACHINE

It should be recognized at the outset that a milling action can be successful only when all machine parts involved are very sturdy and steady. It must be possible for the actual cutting to be done without the slightest vibration caused by overloading or speeding the machine or allowing excessive tolerances between moving machine parts.

The illustration shows only one method to give an idea of what can be done successfully should the need for such an operation become important in the shop.

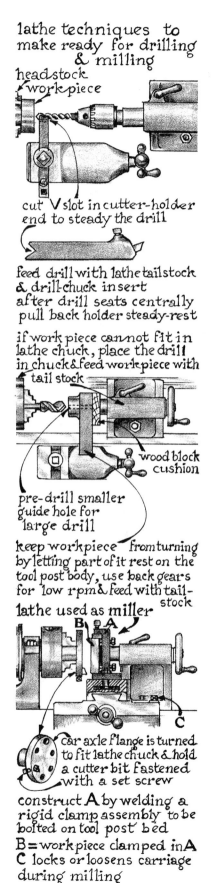

lathe techniques to make ready for drilling & milling

headstock
work piece

cut V slot in cutter-holder end to steady the drill

feed drill with lathe tailstock & drill-chuck insert after drill seats centrally pull back holder steady-rest

if work piece cannot fit in lathe chuck, place the drill in chuck & feed work piece with tail stock

wood block cushion

pre-drill smaller guide hole for large drill

keep workpiece from turning by letting part of it rest on the tool post body, use back gears for low rpm & feed with tail-stock

lathe used as miller
B A

C

car axle flange is turned to fit lathe chuck & hold a cutter bit fastened with a set screw

construct A by welding a rigid clamp assembly to be bolted on tool post bed
B = workpiece clamped in A
C locks or loosens carriage during milling

22. The Trip-Hammer and Its Use

Readers who have not seen a trip-hammer in action should examine carefully the full-page illustration of the one shown here. Observe:

1) How the motions are activated

2) How the rise and fall of the hammer element comes about

3) How to raise or lower the hammer position when the hammer is at rest

4) How the hammer weight is balanced by the flywheel-crank combination

5) The slack or tight belt adjustment, which makes the clutch engage or stop the hammer action to speed it up or slow it down

6) The location of the brake mechanism that releases or stops the lower pulley on the hammer drive shaft

The text and accompanying illustrations are intended to further clarify the workings of the trip-hammer.

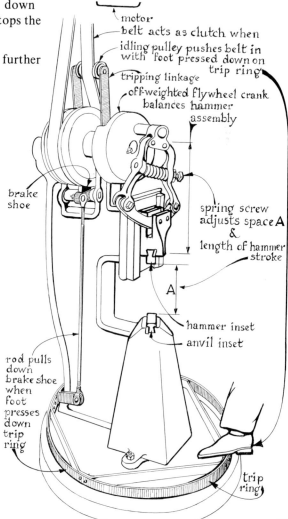

motor
belt acts as clutch when idling pulley pushes belt in with foot pressed down on trip ring
tripping linkage
off-weighted flywheel crank balances hammer assembly
spring screw adjusts space A & length of hammer stroke
brake shoe
A
hammer inset
anvil inset
rod pulls down brake shoe when foot presses down trip ring
trip ring

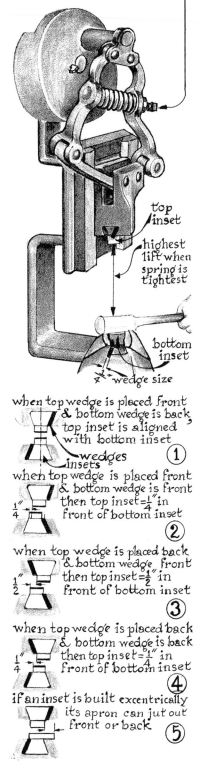

looser spring lowers hammer & tighter spring raises hammer
when spring is looser, hammer speed must be slowed down.
when spring is tightened, the hammer can run faster at a maximum hammer lift

top inset

highest lift when spring is tightest

bottom inset

x wedge size

when top wedge is placed front & bottom wedge is back, top inset is aligned with bottom inset

wedges
insets ①

when top wedge is placed front & bottom wedge is front then top inset = $\frac{1}{4}$" in front of bottom inset

$\frac{1}{4}$" ②

when top wedge is placed back & bottom wedge front then top inset = $\frac{1}{2}$" in front of bottom inset

$\frac{1}{2}$" ③

when top wedge is placed back & bottom wedge is back then top inset = $\frac{1}{4}$" in front of bottom inset

$\frac{1}{4}$" ④

if an inset is built excentrically its apron can jut out front or back ⑤

WHY THE INSET SLOTS ARE OFFSET

The slots are receptacles for the hammer and anvil insets. The offset gives the smith a choice of various inset placements.

The *first diagram* shows a center-to-center alignment of insets. It calls for placing the locking wedges in opposite positions. If the insets are symmetrical it makes the hammer action on the hot workpiece central and symmetrical.

In the *second diagram* the insets are set *unaligned*, with both wedges placed nearest to the smith. In this placement, the workpiece will be indented at the bottom but not at the top when its end is kept flush with the edge of the hammer inset farthest from the smith.

In the *third diagram* the same takes place as in the second, but *shortens* the indentation on the workpiece a little. This wedge positioning gives the smith a chance to forge a local lip at one side of the bar end.

In the *fourth diagram* both wedges are placed on the *far* side of the smith. The insets' positions, in relation to one another, is the same as in the second diagram.

The *fifth diagram* shows that if the smith wants to offset one side of the workpiece longitudinally, he will need an inset with an *extended apron* so that the hammer will strike that portion of the workpiece that rests on the spot directly below the hammer path. The apron then serves as a convenient steady-rest while keeping the bottom of the workpiece unaffected by the hammerblows.

The five diagrams for inset positioning should make it clear that the smith can choose among many inset designs and positionings to suit his plans.

THE FORGING

The illustrations show the positioning of the workpiece, first in the top view of the anvil, and then in the side view between the two insets. Notice that when the two insets are centrally aligned, the edges nearest to the smith are curved somewhat.

Note also that in a long workpiece the portion that protrudes beyond the hammer will bypass the trip-hammer frame because the inset slots have been placed at an angle to the main frame.

If the workpiece is a bar, its heated portion can be steadily pushed forward during the uninterrupted hammering to create a flattened-out portion without leaving sharp indentations in the steel. If that section is moved backward and forward during the hammering, the flattened portions become thinner, longer, and wider.

MOST FREQUENTLY USED INSETS

These are the ones shown in diagrams 1–4. If they are positioned center-to-center and have somewhat rounded edges along the flat facings, they will leave the workpieces with flattened surfaces. Hammering then replaces sledging by a blacksmith's helper.

It is logical that when human helpers became less and less available to the smith he would reach for a trip-hammer to take the helper's place. Without a trip-hammer, sledging frequently *is* needed if the hardest blow the smith can deliver (with the heaviest hammer) is not enough to accomplish what he aims to do. Not only would the smith overtax his strength and endurance, but it would take too much time to finish a given job. When it became possible to produce trip-hammers at a reasonable cost, many a smith looked upon the acquisition of one as a new lease on life. He no longer was dependent on a helper to do sledging. Besides relieving him of the brutal part of the work, he could also make more intricate forgings by designing special insets to meet special shapes. Such insets are referred to as *dies* or *matrixes*. It is that particular aspect of trip-hammer use that proves most useful to the modern smith.

If he has the skill (or can acquire it) to make insets himself, they will help him to make multiples of a single type of workpiece and still stay short of mass-production. Making multiples often holds out the promise that the smith can improve his earnings by doing everything single-handedly.

USING FLAT-FACED INSETS WITH ROUNDED EDGES

The most frequent use of the trip-hammer is for workpieces that need to be *flattened* or *drawn out* in a stretching action. If the facings are perfectly parallel to one another, accurately parallel flat sides can be forged on a bar from thick to thin.

For example, a delicate spatula can be made in seconds and in *one heating* and without using the cross-peen. Resist the temptation, however, to keep on hammering when the visible heat glow has disappeared. The steel is then too cold to change its form further without the danger of cracking.

Remember that the insets are quite cold compared to the hot steel and that the thinner the steel becomes, the greater its surface and the more rapidly it cools despite the enormous amount of energy the heavy hammer pours into it. If the steel becomes too cold for hammering, reheat it before continuing.

One unexpected advantage of the rapid and forceful blows of a trip-hammer is that they increase the quality of the steel; this is especially true in the making of cutting tools. The improvement is caused by the *compacting* of the molecular structure, which the trip-hammer's heavier blows do better than a lighter hammer blow would.

During the final steps in the forging of a carving tool blank, the blade can be compacted deliberately by letting the last blows, before the blade gets too cool, be the heaviest and fastest. This is referred to as *packing* the steel.

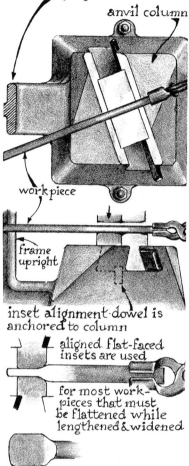

anvil inset slot is angled with column top to allow long workpieces to clear the frame upright

anvil column

workpiece

frame upright

inset alignment-dowel is anchored to column

aligned flat-faced insets are used

for most work-pieces that must be flattened while lengthened & widened

MAKING WEDGES

To make a heavy wedge, the stock of a salvaged car axle will do very well.

First cut off the hub and flange part of the axle. The remaining length, about 24 inches, can then conveniently be hand held during the forging.

The first skill to acquire in using the trip-hammer is holding the workpiece in exact alignment with the anvil inset facings. As a rule, this is at right angles with the path of the hammer. Accurate holding of the workpiece prevents its bending out of line during forging. It also prevents the often painful jerk in the hands that hold the end of the workpiece. This happens at its worst when heavy-gauge stock is held inaccurately and when it becomes a little too cold to continue forging. (If the part to be forged is at *yellow heat*, inaccurate holding bends it out of line without much strain on the hands.)

Begin forging the wedge with *medium blows*, increasing them in force while gradually drawing the workpiece toward you. When you have reached the very tip, commence all over again where that section is thickest, hammering with medium blows and increasing them gradually to *forceful* ones, again drawing the workpiece toward you to its very tip. In this way you forge the graduated thickness required for a wedge.

By working steadily and quickly with forceful blows, you will be able to keep the workpiece at forging heat. Much of the heat loss is compensated for by heavy hammerblows converted into heat, thus slowing the rate at which the workpiece cools off. Keep in mind with any forging you do that forceful hammerblows *add heat* to the workpiece.

When making wedges, the thinner part of the wedge becomes broader in time, making it necessary to forge its sides together intermittently if a parallel wedge is wanted. If the slope of the insets is not too steep, you can forge the sides of the wedge approximately without having to change the insets. Or you can parallel the sides from time to time by hand-forging on the anvil.

HAMMER TEXTURE ON THE WORKPIECE

If the workpiece must be smooth and free from indentations left by the somewhat rounded edges of the insets, the inset design will have to be changed somewhat. This is done by *sloping* upward the hammer inset face nearest the smith and rounding it slightly. If the anvil inset remains horizontal, no local indentations will result.

The workpiece is held the same way as before, at right angles with the hammer path. If only the anvil inset face slopes downward toward the smith, he should lower his hands somewhat, holding the workpiece to even out the effect of each inset facing on it during hammering. If *both* inset faces slope outward toward the smith, he can again position the workpiece at right angles with the hammer path as was done when both insets had facings parallel to each other.

In whatever combination the insets are arranged, the workpiece should be pushed back and forth gradually during the hammering while the tripping-foot control directs harder or lighter blows, slower or faster, as the smith judges is required.

CORRECTIVE HAMMERING

Watching closely how the *yellow hot* steel shapes up during the hammering tells you immediately where and how you must place the heated bar to get what you are after, or to correct what you did wrong. In spite of the accuracy of machine action, some differences do show up if the workpiece is held a little off dead center of the hammer path. If the center of the workpiece is not in the exact center of the hammer inset it seems as though the entire machine structure *gives* somewhat, one way or the other.

If the trip-hammer is an old, worn one, these differences will show up more, but, strange to say, good use can be made of such flexibility if you wish to use only the right or the left part of the hammer during corrective hammering. Having worked with worn trip-hammers a great deal, I find that their loose-jointed action becomes almost an advantage, giving me an additional choice of workpiece placement.

MAKING INSETS TO FORM TAPER ENDINGS ON RODS

Clamp two inset blanks together and drill a hole at the center where the two faces meet. Next grind each inset separately, as shown, to form an approximate cone shape. It must end up well-rounded at the end edges. Both insets are centrally aligned to receive the round stock at the larger part of the cone that faces the smith.

During the hammering, feed the *yellow hot* stock forward gradually between the insets, rotating the rod continuously. This squeezes the steel so that it develops a circular, rather than an oval, profile as each hammerblow counteracts somewhat the oval profile created by the previous blow. Toward the end the force of the blows should be tapered off while the piece is worked backward and forward, and rotated all the while. The result will be remarkably accurate as your manipulation becomes more and more skillful.

VARIATIONS

The illustration shows how to position a round rod, heated locally about one or two inches from the end. Continuously rotate the rod during the hammering; when it reaches the desired size and dimension, gradually push the workpiece forward to position 2, hammering all the while; end up finally with position 3, rotating the rod around its own axis all the while. A taper with a *round shoulder section* results. This shape is the first step in making a wood gouge blank.

The untouched end can be widened for the gouge blade, first with the peen of the hammer, and then flattened between the flat-faced insets of the trip-hammer. It is up to you when peening must be done; you may choose instead to spend the time changing insets for this purpose and afterwards replace the flat-faced insets and smooth the widened blade section.

Making a wide blade from a larger diameter stock with a trip-hammer eliminates the need to upset lighter stock for the blade, thus saving time and effort. It is practical to start with heavier stock, since the drawing-out and peening of steel with the trip-hammer takes only a little time and the least physical effort.

Two- and Three-step Insets

The illustrations show insets that have a choice between two seating profiles instead of one. This allows the smith to make long, slender tapers more easily. The first profile has the larger diameter seating, which permits forging of a shorter, stubbier taper. After reheating, the taper can be made more slender in the smaller profile next to it.

Special Insets

If specific blanks are needed for *quantity forgings*, insets must be made that can shape various cross sections of workpieces more easily than if they were forged by hand. It is here that the time spent on making special insets becomes justified.

The most frequent cross section of salvaged stock is *square* or *round*. With the insets shown, a round is first hammered out into a triangle bed with cross sections that are fairly deep. The resulting

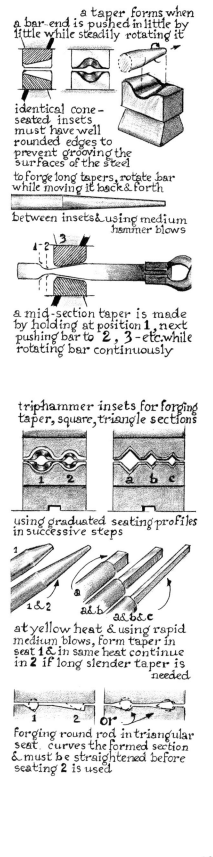

a taper forms when a bar-end is pushed in little by little while steadily rotating it

identical cone-seated insets must have well rounded edges to prevent grooving the surfaces of the steel

to forge long tapers, rotate bar while moving it back & forth between insets & using medium hammer blows

a mid-section taper is made by holding at position 1, next pushing bar to 2, 3 -etc.while rotating bar continuously

triphammer insets for forging taper, square, triangle sections

using graduated seating profiles in successive steps

at yellow heat & using rapid medium blows, form taper in seat 1 & in same heat continue in 2 if long slender taper is needed

forging round rod in triangular seat curves the formed section & must be straightened before seating 2 is used

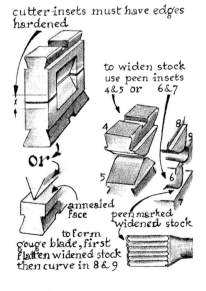

hammer out thick stock to size for thin knife blades

engravers' burin

draw knife

trim blanks with file & or motor grinders, sanders, polishers before hardening & tempering

forging, when reheated, is placed in the *next shallower* profile. It will then fill it completely, producing a triangular stock for making small knives or engraver's burins. With a little practice, you will be able to forge such stock without curving it, (curving being a natural tendency when a bar is stretched on one side more than the other).

CUTOFF INSETS

These can do what cutoff *hardies* do on the anvil. The power of the trip-hammer makes it possible to cut heavy-gauge stock without great effort. The insets must do the cutting without ruining the sharpened knife edge. To do this, each knife section ending must be flat-faced and at the same level as the knife edge. The final blow that cuts the stock in two will fall at the point where the flat-faced endings meet and the knife edges barely touch one another.

Another method is to leave the bottom inset annealed for cutting purposes. In this instance, a *hardened hammer inset* edge cuts the stock the moment it starts cutting into the annealed surface of the anvil inset.

WARNING: There is a real danger that the severed part of the stock will, at that moment, fly off at high speed. It could hit a bystander or start a fire should it land in combustible material.

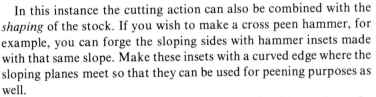

cutter insets must have edges hardened

to widen stock use peen insets 4 & 5 or 6 & 7

or

annealed face

peen marked widened stock

to form gouge blade, first flatten widened stock then curve in 8 & 9

A Third Way of Cutting Stock

In this instance the cutting action can also be combined with the *shaping* of the stock. If you wish to make a cross peen hammer, for example, you can forge the sloping sides with hammer insets made with that same slope. Make these insets with a curved edge where the sloping planes meet so that they can be used for peening purposes as well.

If sections of car axles are cut with this pair of insets, keep the *yellow hot* part firmly in position while the hardest and fastest hammerblows bring the curved endings of the insets together, leaving a very thin connecting link that holds the stock together. At that point, stop the action and knock off the end piece over the anvil or pry it off with tongs. In this way, the hot piece will not fly off uncontrolled.

I practice this method for making hammer heads with good results on my own trip-hammer. It has saved much effort and time compared with hand-hammering a cross peen separately on the anvil.

SWAGES AND FULLERS

Almost all accessories for hand-hammering on an anvil can be duplicated as trip-hammer insets, functioning as top and bottom swages and top and bottom fullers.

23. Making a Pair of Insets to Forge a Gouge Blade

Most of the difficulties encountered in hand-forging a wood-carving gouge can be overcome with a trip-hammer. In the design of the gouge shown here, the shank and the bottom of the blade form a straight line. In hand-forging it is difficult to force the thicker part of the blade down to the point at which it meets the shank without distorting that part. There is the danger that the thinner areas of the steel will give way under hammerblows much sooner than the stiffer, thicker parts.

In order to curve the blade at the point where it is narrowest, yet thickest, a heavy blow must be struck on that spot with a matching curved hammer forcing it down onto the flat facing of the anvil. Failing to do so correctly causes the bottom profile of the tool blank to hump up at that thickest point. To meet this difficulty when hand-forging, place the heated blank with the bottom profile on the flat anvil face. Hold the ball of an appropriate size ball peen hammer on the hump and strike its face with a hammer to force the hump down flush with the anvil face. As a rule, one or two such treatments will correct the discrepancy. Only after the blank is correctly aligned can the shape of the blade ending be refined.

"Humping up" can be avoided from the start with specially designed trip-hammer insets that shape a gouge blank with the proper alignment. The *bottom inset* can be made by joining two pieces of steel as shown for insets A and B. Should you possess a piece of steel large enough to make the unit out of one piece, by all means do so. But since the inset apron falls outside the hammer's path, very little force is transplanted by the workpiece onto the apron. In fact, the apron serves more or less as a steady-rest, easing the smith's manipulation during forging and allowing him to keep the workpiece in perfect alignment, holding it firmly seated in that bottom rest during hammering.

Working the blank backward and forward a bit will permit you to feel when the most forward position has been reached, the point at which the thickest part of the blade meets the shank. A few firm hammerblows on that spot will seat it flush with the shank bottom. You can now pull the blank *toward* you again until the top inset reaches the very edge of the gouge blade ending. If the blade is still hot enough, you can end up using the most forceful hammerblows to *pack* the steel.

It may appear at first glance at the illustrations that making such an inset unit is too difficult. But if you can visualize the step-by-step procedure, you will see that making each part is actually rather simple. If you feel, therefore, that the gain outweighs any difficulty you might encounter in making the unit, I strongly recommend that you do so.

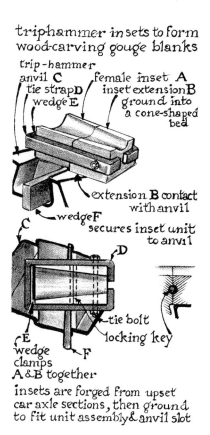

triphammer insets to form wood-carving gouge blanks

trip-hammer anvil **C**
tie strap **D**
wedge **E**
female inset **A**
inset extension **B** ground into a cone-shaped bed

extension **B** contact with anvil

C — wedge **F** secures inset unit to anvil

D

tie bolt locking key

E wedge clamps A & B together **F**

insets are forged from upset car axle sections, then ground to fit unit assembly & anvil slot

95

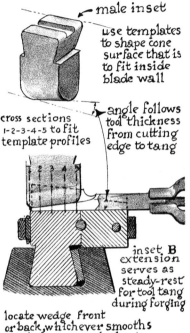

— male inset

use templates to shape cone surface that is to fit inside blade wall

cross sections 1-2-3-4-5 to fit template profiles

angle follows tool thickness from cutting edge to tang

inset **B** extension serves as steady-rest for tool tang during forging

locate wedge front or back, whichever smooths out hammer marks best

template profiles

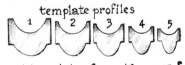

cut templates from tin cans & refine curves to match the previously hand-forged tool blank

Making the *top inset* is an entirely different matter. I suggest that you avoid making hammer insets with horizontal extensions. The extension can cause enormous strains on the machinery as a whole, particularly if the extreme outward part of it hits the bottom inset unintentionally with full force. The effect would be to wrench the moving parts of the machinery to the breaking point. Do not underestimate the enormous forces that come into play when a rapidly moving hammer mass releases its stored energy upon impact with the anvil inset. The hammer inset must, therefore, be allowed to distribute its energy within the range for which it is designed. It must not fall beyond the projected area of the hammer body itself.

The hammer inset should be designed to fill the inner space of the finished blade of the gouge so that, in the end, a full contact is established between the workpiece and both inset walls. The illustrations show how to accomplish this. Examine the cross sections of the hammer insets; they match the curvature of several templates you can make.

Use a hand-forged finished tool as a *model* to make the insets. First, fit the *bottom inset* depressions exactly along the curves of the templates. (As shown in the illustration as profiles 1–5.) Next, use the templates to fit the *hammer inset* curves.

If made well, the two insets will allow sufficient steel between them to shape the blank correctly at the moment the surfaces of both insets contact it. Make certain that the edges at each end of the hammer inset are rounded off so that at no time can local depressions mar the blade blank beyond repair.

After both insets have been installed, position the hammer at its lowest so that the small space between them allows you to check the center-to-center alignment. If the insets prove to be unaligned after they have been wedged in, when hot steel is hammered between them the offset hammerblow would immediately result in sideways forging. The blade would then become much thinner on one side than on the other and would also curve out of line. The location of the error itself will indicate in which direction inset positions must be corrected to establish a perfect center-to-center alignment.

Only when you have mastered correct positioning of these two insets will using them become a joy. They will cut time in half or better when you make such carving tool blanks on the trip-hammer.

It is at this point that you have a choice: Shall you leave well enough alone, having reaped the benefit of a quickly and beautifully forged blade section of a gouge, and go on to hand-forge the rest (shank, shoulder and tang)? Or should you attempt to make additional insets for the trip-hammer with which to shape the remaining parts of the tool? It is a critical decision to make. The temptation to mechanize further is great. We all fall prey to it at one time or another, overreaching ourselves without being aware that we are doing so.

Making insets for complicated workpieces is bound to take time. Sometimes we make mistakes and must do the work all over again. In general, my advice is that, with limited equipment, it is preferable to *combine* the trip-hammer with some hand-forging. The remaining sections are really not too difficult to forge by hand. You can accomplish what you set out to do: to make multiples, short of mass production, within time limits that are acceptable to the independent, self-employed smith.

24. Making Trip-Hammer Insets From Trolley Rail

Once you have learned to operate the trip-hammer using simple insets, the next step is to make additional ones from easily available varieties of scrap steel. Small-gauge trolley rail is one suitable item that can often be found. Its T-shaped cross section will need to be built up from below so that the finished inset units can be anchored in the hammer and anvil slots.

It would be overreaching to try to fill the open spaces with steel sections, especially since hardwood sections will do as well. No excessive heat ever reaches the wood, so there is no danger of it burning. Using hardwood props simplifies making trip-hammer insets from odd-profiled bulky scrap steel, especially if that material is a high-carbon steel that can be tempered to the exact hardness we want.

The step-by-step procedure illustrated shows a simple way of installing these insets. Treat them as if they were made from one solid piece of steel. The only difficulty is making the matrix parts of the insets by forging methods. It is possible that you will find in your own shop a simpler way of doing what has been suggested here. The perfect results that I have obtained do, however, justify the somewhat laborious task of making the male and female parts of these insets.

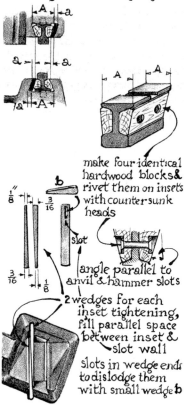

using sections of scrap rail in the making of inset units for trip-hammer projects
Example: a wood gouge

make four identical hardwood blocks & rivet them on insets with countersunk heads

angle parallel to anvil & hammer slots

2 wedges for each inset tightening, fill parallel space between inset & slot wall

slots in wedge ends to dislodge them with small wedge **b**

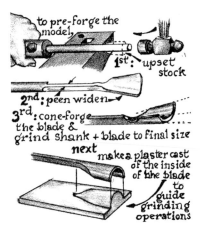

to pre-forge the model,

1st: upset stock

2nd: peen widen

3rd: cone-forge the blade & grind shank + blade to final size

next makes a plaster cast of the inside of the blade to guide grinding operations

THE INSET DIES

The plan for forging a carving gouge blank is that only the tool *blade* and *shank* are to be shaped on the trip-hammer.

First, hand-forge a *model tool* to be copied in making the inset dies for the gouge blade and shank. Finish all parts of the tool until you are satisfied with the shape and design.

Making the Top Inset Die

Using the model tool, cast an impression of the *hollow part* of the blade and shank in plaster of Paris. This form can then be duplicated in steel to make the *top inset*.

NOTE: When two opposite parts, as in male and female dies, must be made, we think of one as being *positive* and the other *negative*; or one being solid and the other hollow. The opposites fit together like a pudding and the pudding mold. If we look at the parts separately, but must *visualize* the two fitting together, a confusing "mirror" effect often results in our making the forms the *opposite* of what they should be. It is the mirror that makes of our *real* right side a left side when we look into it. Be on guard against this mirror switch. Making a plaster cast is a good way to avoid the difficulty. If you duplicate the cast of the *tool* precisely, the result will be the correct *inset* shape.

To make that inset, use as tools anything in the shop that is suitable. Filing, hacking, grinding, and hammering are all permissible as long as you can reach the narrow recesses without breaking fragile tools.

The Correct Use of Grinding Points

The grinding points should be *exactly centered* and *exactly round* before a grinding operation begins. If they are eccentric, the procedure to restore accuracy is simple: Hold the rotating grinding point driven by the high-speed grinding unit (gently but steadily) against the rotating surface of the large, coarse, hard grinding wheel so that the rotation of both tends to grind away every trace of eccentricity of the small point.

While you are at it, such small points may be further shaped by the big wheel into whatever profile you may want. Small wheels and grinding points are not expensive and all of them can be reshaped for special jobs.

I find that grinding points at high rpm in hand-held, motor-driven grinders are most useful *after* the bulk of the material has been removed with larger tools.

WARNING: High-speed grinders can be dangerous instruments if overloaded because of misjudgment or lack of skill in controlling their manipulation. If the grinding point grabs the steel, it may fly apart. The danger is that sections can injure the operator or bystanders if no protective shields are used. Wear safety goggles at all times when doing this type of work.

Testing the Final Surface of the Inset for Accuracy

Coat the surface of the model with a little blacking. Place it in or over the inset matrix surface and wiggle it in that position. Lift it off and examine the surface of matrix for telltale black spots left by the

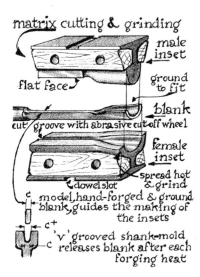

matrix cutting & grinding

male inset

flat face

ground to fit

blank

cut groove with abrasive cut-off wheel

female inset

dowel slot

spread hot & grind

model, hand-forged & ground blank, guides the making of the insets

'v' grooved shank-mold releases blank after each forging heat

model. These indicate where more grinding must be done. Continue to grind and test until an overall *even* marking of black contact areas is achieved. This shows that the form surface fits exactly its opposite.

Shaping the Bottom Inset

Heat the *anvil* part of the inset *yellow hot*. Clamp it into the post blacksmith vise and hammer that part of the yellow hot groove wall *outward* with a blunt-ended bar in the approximate shape of the gouge blade contour. Anneal the inset so that the steel will be at its softest.

Next, do the machining by every means available—filing, hacking, hand-grinding. Finally, test with the gouge model to see whether the job has been done accurately.

Tempering

Harden the trip-hammer insets in oil. The resulting soft core is desirable because it will cushion the hardened surfaces against breaking. And if hardened surfaces should crack, the outer part will not shatter because the softer center holds the broken parts together.

As a rule, such cracks are shallow and remain insignificant during further use of the tool. Nonetheless, the cracks may show that you have hardened the piece more than necessary or that the inset was overloaded by accident when a powerful hammerblow struck the hard anvil inset face without any soft-heated steel between the two. This also makes a good case for reheating steel that has cooled off too much, since heavy hammering of cold, hard steel has a similar effect on the insets to striking the empty anvil face itself.

TROUBLESHOOTING

There are various types and makes of trip-hammers, and their owners have to develop a skill to operate them within the limits of their designs and capability. Using trip-hammers and making insets for them sometimes introduces unforeseen difficulties. These show up in faulty end results or accidents. Following is a discussion of what are, in my experience, the most frequent mishaps and what steps can be taken to avoid trouble.

The Insets Become Loosened

During forceful hammering the insets may loosen, but this frequently is not noticed in time because the noise of the operation drowns out the telltale sounds of a loose wedge. If that wedge should drop out of the hammer slot before you can stop the hammer, it can fall free onto the lower inset. The next hammerblow by the *empty hammer body* would then hit whatever part lies below it. There is a great danger that something will be irreparably damaged by such impact.

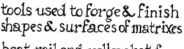

tools used to forge & finish shapes & surfaces of matrixes

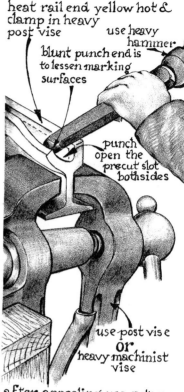

heat rail end yellow hot & clamp in heavy post vise

use heavy hammer.

blunt punch end is to lessen marking surfaces

punch open the precut slot both sides

use post vise or heavy machinist vise

after annealing, use rotary files, drum sanders, grinding points to refine pre-forged & cut shapes

flexible grinding disc in electric drill chuck

rotary file

high speed hand-held electric grinder

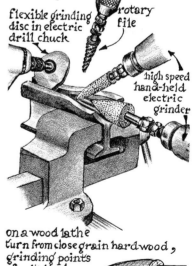

on a wood lathe turn from close grain hardwood, grinding points of suitable shapes & held in drill chuck at slow rpm, refine with lapping compound all final surfaces. next surfaces can be smoothed further with tripoli on cotton buffers

harden at bronze temper color

The Wedges Become Loosened

Be sure to provide the seatings with a correct slant to match the wedge. If insets do not have the right wedge seatings, there is a great chance that the wedges will loosen during hammering. Do not consider that you have finished making an inset until you have ensured that the wedges anchor it securely.

Tips for Aligning Insets

Insets *must* be correctly aligned before good results can be expected. If your sighting ability is inadequate and you require measuring instruments, use calipers or any other measuring device to make certain that both insets are perfectly aligned when they have to be, and accurately offset when the design calls for that.

If the position of the insets should be misaligned sideways due to excessive clearance between the centering dowel pin and the inset's own seating slot, a little trick can often correct it. Install the male and female insets but leave the wedges slightly *loose* during the first two or three hammerblows. Hold a strip of thick, stiff cardboard, instead of hot steel, between the insets. The sideways forces during the blows will tend to automatically move the two insets into alignment. If indentations left on the cardboard by these hammerblows show an *even bearing* right and left, it means that the trick succeeded, and the wedges can then be tightened.

If the indentations show only on *one side*, the inset position must be examined and relocated somewhat. Do this by making more room to one side of the seating, using a rotary file as a milling cutter; make up for the excess clearance on the other side with a *filler strip*. If you have the use of an acetylene torch, a few blobs of melted metal will do instead of a filler strip.

Pocking of Inset Facings

Inset facings that have not been hardened correctly will in due time show pockmarked surfaces, which in turn leave uneven surfaces on the forged workpiece. Regrinding and smoothing all contact areas and then correctly hardening them should solve the problem.

25. Trip-Hammer Upsetting

Upsetting steel with the trip-hammer offers an improvement over upsetting by hand only if the machine can eliminate the human errors in hand-hammering and hand-holding.

Since hand-holding must be done in *either* case, trip-hammer manipulation can meet the problem only halfway. Cup-shaped anvil and hammer insets can be made and used to center the workpiece automatically. The illustrations show how it is accomplished.

In practice, however, even the slightest unaligned hand-holding requires that the smith continually move the workpiece around its own vertical axis in order to compensate for previous inaccurate positioning. The illustrations show how to prevent bending the workpiece during upsetting.

To prevent further sideways bending, the workpiece should be cooled by a quick immersion of 1/4 inch of each end in water for a second or more before placing the piece in vertical alignment between trip-hammer insets. Rapid hammering, combined with circular holding movements, will then upset the middle part and not the ends.

Once that midsection has become thick enough to resist outward bending, replace both cup insets with flat-faced ones. Now the piece can easily be upset into a short, thick cylinder to make, for example, a hammer blank, as shown.

Making a Hammer Head

First drill a 1/4-inch diameter hole at the center of the blank, which you made by upsetting the axle section as shown before. This acts as a guide for the cone-head fullers, which will be hammered into it to enlarge it to fit the size hammer stem you want.

CAUTION: The guide hole must run through the dead center of the blank, not to either side. Otherwise the cone fuller will spread the metal on the thinner side more than on the other, which would weaken that side as well as placing the hammer stem hole still further out of center.

If you intend to locate the center by eye, it is best to clamp the workpiece in the drill vise and, bringing your line of sight level with it, visualize the extension of the drill as it bisects the circle. After the drill has entered the steel 1/8 inch, resight the position and make whatever correction may be needed. In this way, you can establish acceptable accuracy without measuring instruments.

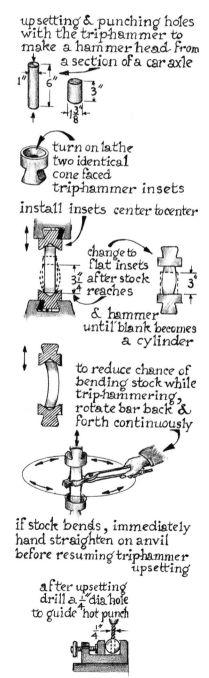

upsetting & punching holes with the triphammer to make a hammer head from a section of a car axle

1" 6" 3" 1 3/8"

turn on lathe two identical cone faced triphammer insets

install insets center to center

change to flat insets after stock 3 3/4" reaches & hammer until blank becomes a cylinder   3"

to reduce chance of bending stock while trip-hammering, rotate bar back & forth continuously

if stock bends, immediately hand straighten on anvil before resuming triphammer upsetting

after upsetting drill a 1/4" dia hole to guide hot punch

1/4"

Correcting an Off-center Guide Hole

In the event that the guide hole is drilled off center, the recommended method of correction is as follows:

Keep the thinner side as cool as possible short of brittle hardness so that when the cone fuller is introduced the steel on the thin side will not stretch as much as the thicker, hot side will.

This is a difficult procedure and there is a danger of ruining the workpiece. Care should, therefore, be taken to drill accurately to begin with.

Finishing the Blank for Final Shaping

After the cone-head fullers have widened the hole sufficiently at top and bottom, a narrower channel is left between the two. This is desirable since it will hold the hammer stem securely at the point it most needs to be. A steel wedge driven into the top end of the hammer stem will spread the wood, locking the stem into place.

At *yellow heat* forge the blank between flat-faced hammer insets, as shown. This automatically reshapes the hole into an oval.

It is now up to the smith to decide the type of hammer head he wishes to make. He can end up with a cross peen, a ball peen, or other shapes useful to him.

The surfaces can then be refined by grinding, filing, turning on a lathe. Finally, such a hammer head should be tempered as explained in Chapter 6.

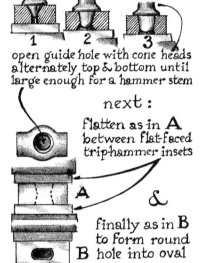

open guide hole with cone heads alternately top & bottom until large enough for a hammer stem

next :

flatten as in A between flat-faced triphammer insets

A

&

finally as in B to form round B hole into oval

26. Insets Made from Car Axle Flange Endings

Sometimes certain types of scrap steel parts come our way in such quantity that it is a challenge to the imagination to create something from such a windfall. That was the case when I fell heir to several hundred pounds of fine quality *steel discs*, 3/8 inch thick by 2, 3, and 4 inches in diameter.

The first idea that came to my mind was to forge deep cup-shapes which, in turn, could be forged into rosettes. Large, heavy-gauge rosettes can be used as giant washers for bolt heads on the long tie rods used to keep building walls securely spaced. The same type of rosette, being heavy, can also serve as a base for a lamp or candlestick (see Chapter 3) or a column that holds an arm with a magnifying glass. In short, the discs have become valuable stock in my shop and have been put to many other uses also.

MAKING INSETS TO FORGE INTO CUP SHAPES

Car axle ends have enough bulk to make a ball inset. First, cut off the hub section from the car axle. Next, using the lathe, cut off the flange at the hub end, since the ball bearing cannot be removed with the flange in the way.

Hold the remnant between the jaws of the heavy post vise so that the edges of the press-fit ball bearing rest on them. With a few, very heavy hammerblows on the stub shaft, drive the ball bearing off its seating. You may need to use a sledge hammer, but in that case the vise must be of a very heavy caliber, 100 pounds at least.

The end of the hub body frequently has a deep depression, which can be filled with a tight-fitting lug in order to make the best use of the greatest volume of hub steel. To make certain that the plug will not drop out during use as a hammer inset, taper the plug slightly so that the larger part of it fits the bottom of the depression in the hub end.

With the cold plug held in readiness, heat the hub body collar around the depression to a *yellow heat*, quickly insert the cold, tapered plug, and hammer the hub until all clearances around the plug are closed. Cool all slowly in an annealing action. This assembly will behave as if it had a solid head.

Next, clamp the blank into the lathe's three-jaw chuck, as shown, and turn the end into a *ball shape* with the regular cutter bits. Finally, refine it with a special cutter made for this project, as illustrated on page 86.

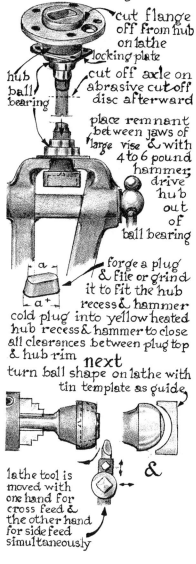

trip-hammer insets made of car axle flange ends

cut flange off from hub on lathe

locking plate

hub ball bearing

cut off axle on abrasive cut-off disc afterward

place remnant between jaws of large vise & with 4 to 6 pound hammer, drive hub out of ball bearing

forge a plug & file or grind it to fit the hub recess & hammer cold plug into yellow heated hub recess & hammer to close all clearances between plug top & hub rim next turn ball shape on lathe with tin template as guide

lathe tool is moved with one hand for cross feed & the other hand for side feed simultaneously

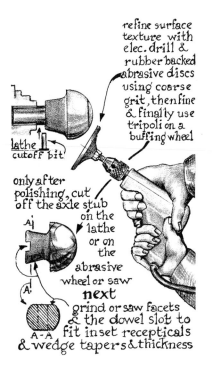

refine surface texture with elec. drill & rubber backed abrasive discs using coarse grit, then fine & finally use tripoli on a buffing wheel

lathe cutoff bit

only after polishing, cut off the axle stub on the lathe or on the abrasive wheel or saw

next

grind or saw facets & the dowel slot to fit inset recepticals & wedge tapers & thickness

A-A

Making the Bowl-shaped Anvil Inset

Trial and error is often the quickest method when using items available from the scrap pile. If scrap articles are too light to withstand the great strains insets must take under forging, they must be reinforced to prevent distortion.

Heat a second car axle hub, from which the bowl-shaped lower inset is to be made, to *yellow heat*. Clamp it in the vise and, with the heavy ball peen hammer, enlarge the depression until it becomes round and bowl-shaped. Its small diameter below the bowl needs to rest on a 1/2-inch-thick washer to bridge the slot opening in the anvil and to cushion the inset base against distortion during hammering. The washer may have to be turned on the lathe.

Cut off the excess axle section and cut the inset base into a profile to fit the standard wedging arrangement. The illustrations show the two assemblies ready to be installed for making cup shapes out of the flat round discs.

Examine the illustration in which an inset rim is reinforced by a crimped-on rim around it.

FORGING A CUP SHAPE OUT OF A FLAT DISC

Instead of trying to hold the heated disc centered over the inset bowl with tong-type tools, you may find the system I have devised a better solution.

The Hold-down Tool

Use a bar 1/4 inch by 3 inches by 10 inches. Heat one end *yellow hot* and place it over the center of the bowl-shaped anvil inset. A few blows with the ball inset hammer will shape the end of the flat bar into a cup.

This cold hold-down tool is intended to be held on a centrally positioned, flat, hot disc over the bowl anvil inset and to be hammered into the hot disc. It forms the disc into a cup shape. Examine the illustrations carefully, noting the sequence for making these cup shapes.

The hold-down tool should be firmly pressed down by hand onto the hot disc, guiding it this way and that, slanting and correcting its position during the hammering. You will quickly develop a skill in manipulating the tool until it seems to center itself as the cup begins to fill the depression of the bowl inset.

Save the final blows for a second heating, before which you should clean the bottom of the inset bowl of accumulated oxidation scales and coal dust. The final hammering on the reheated shaped cup in the cleaned bowl inset will yield an accurate and smooth finish if the ball inset also is smooth and accurate.

The finished cup will need a bit of additional work on the lathe if you want machine accuracy. To do this, anneal the cup and clamp it in the lathe. Turn the inside of the bowl with a tool especially made for it, as shown in the illustration in Chapter 21.

To machine the outside of the cup, spread the chuck jaws in the cup that is placed over the jaw tips. Hold it in that position with the tail-center point pressed onto the cup's center. After the cup rim is machined, it can be clamped between the chuck jaws and finished further with the large, circular cutter shown in the illustration on page 86.

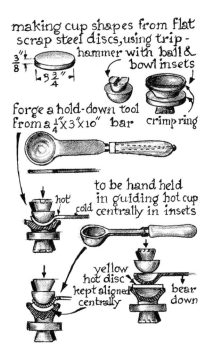

making cup shapes from flat scrap steel discs, using trip-hammer with ball & bowl insets

3/8"t
9 3/4"

forge a hold-down tool from a 1/4"x 3"x 10" bar

crimp ring

to be hand held in guiding hot cup centrally in insets

hot
cold

yellow hot disc kept aligned centrally

bear down

MAKING LARGE ROSETTES WITH THE TRIP-HAMMER

Locate a heavy, solid piece of scrap from which to make another inset. Turn it on the lathe into a receptacle for one of the already forged blanks. Its diameter should be *half* that of the cup.

On the lathe turn an *outside ring* that can be slipped over the circular inset, as shown, to act as a guide to keep the cup blank from wandering sideways.

The next item needed is a *flat set-hammer*, made by riveting a head onto two 3/8-inch-thick scrap discs to give it the needed stiffness. This is intended to slip easily inside the guide ring and rest on top of the heated, open-faced cup blank.

With the heated cup blank in position below it, the set-hammer is then hammered down with the trip-hammer. This flattens the free portion of the cup blank onto the flat, marginal, circular face of the anvil inset.

The workpiece is now a circular base with a marginal flange and a high, curved hump in the middle. It is around this hump that deep scallops are forged to make a decorative rosette.

The scallops can be made with hand-held ball heads that are hammered down with the trip-hammer while the heated marginal flange is held with tongs between the flat-faced top and bottom inset.

The illustration also shows a tool to create toe-holds for the ball head on the flange surface. These preliminary indentations are made with the same hammerblows that make the marginal flange. You next use ball heads to create an end result that looks entirely handmade. This is because that last hand-directed placement of various sizes of ball heads removes every trace of a mass-produced machine-made article.

Surface Treatments for the Finished Rosette

The appearance of such a rosette can be enhanced through different surface finishes. It can be steel-brushed, then heated up a little before applying warm linseed oil, which will fill the tiniest pores in the surface. This produces the black finish typical of forged steel.

Another surface treatment is to move the rosette surface against a rotating rubber-backed, fine grit, abrasive disc, allowing this flexible disc to rub over the protrusions of the rosette surface but not to reach its valleys. The result is that the ridges show as silver in contrast to the black, bringing out the texture sharply.

Follow up this treatment by holding the rosette surface against a tripoli-impregnated buffer. The silver ridges become highly polished, but the black depressions are left unaffected.

It is now important to clean the wax residue from the surface with turpentine or comparable solvent. Next heat the whole over the blue flame of a gas burner; the kitchen stove burner will do. Wait for oxidation colors to appear, stopping the process by quenching the whole in water when the color is to your liking.

The rosette can be sprayed with an acrylic fixitive to extend the lifetime of the patinated surface and to protect it against erosion. Once you have become proficient at such surface-treating and coloring, your end results will have a jewel-like appearance.

The completed rosette is ideally suited for a variety of uses. For instance, it can be used as a heavy base for the column of a candlestick a lamp, or as any object to be held in a stable position. Rosettes can also, of course, be used as decorative ornaments.

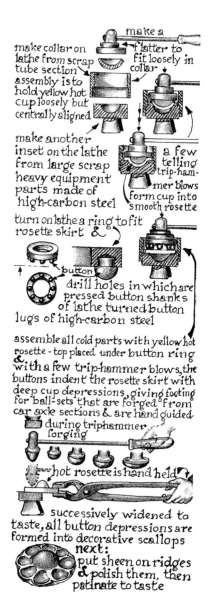

make a flatter to fit loosely in collar

make collar on lathe from scrap tube section assembly is to hold yellow hot cup loosely but centrally aligned

make another inset on the lathe from large scrap heavy equipment parts made of high-carbon steel

a few telling trip-hammer blows form cup into smooth rosette

turn on lathe a ring to fit rosette skirt &

button

drill holes in which are pressed button shanks of lathe turned button lugs of high-carbon steel

assemble all cold parts with yellow hot rosette - top placed under button ring & with a few trip-hammer blows, the buttons indent the rosette skirt with deep cup depressions, giving footing for ball-sets that are forged from car axle sections & are hand guided during triphammer forging

hot rosette is hand held

successively widened to taste, all button depressions are formed into decorative scallops

next: put sheen on ridges & polish them, then patinate to taste

27. Sharpening Tool Edges

ⓑ *to* ⓐ resharpen with strop only.

ⓐ = thickness of burr

stropped surface

microscopic view of final edge anything thinner than ⓐ will bend or break, no matter how perfect the temper

testing for sharpness

right way to detect burr

fine grit or hone

burr

leather strop

final honed sharp edge

cotton buffing wheels

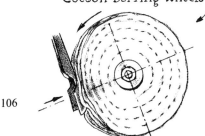

It is necessary that the student first visualize what takes place at a tool's edge when it is ground for sharpness.

The angle at that edge where the two sides meet is a line of intersection of two planes. Mathematically, the dimension at that point is zero. It means that its cutting edge would have in actuality no dimension; hence, strength is absent. This visualization is at first difficult to comprehend. But in geometry, when two lines are shown intersecting *on paper*, it is easily understood.

It is the microscopic size of the sharp edge, then, that we must deal with—a size that approaches zero. At the same time it must remain strong enough to withstand the strain during the cutting action. This is our basic concern in sharpening all cutting tool edges.

Therefore, if that microscopic edge is made slightly *rounded* it will mean that its final size is *more* than absolute zero, giving it enough strength to withstand bending while cutting smoothly.

If you find it difficult to visualize this minuteness, consider the notion of engraving the Lord's Prayer on the head of a pin. Minuteness is somewhat easier to comprehend thanks to electron microscope photography. It can show us the gigantic-looking forms of hair on the surface of the almost invisible eyes of insects; it can show us body cells, bacteria, viruses, atoms.

The illustration shows the enlarged portion of a tool edge. When, during grinding, zero dimension is approached, the thin steel will bend away under the pressure of the grinding stone. Then the grit no longer cuts, but *slides* off the steel, forming a *feather edge*.

That feather or *burr* must be removed. If it were not, it would fold over during cutting, and would buckle, break or tear off, leaving a row of microscopic, jagged teeth. In use, the tool would drag and tear, instead of *shearing* the material, leaving a ruptured texture instead of a smooth one. The solution is to *strop* the edge on a leather strop like the ones barbers used to sharpen their razors.

A MODERN METHOD OF "STROPPING" TOOL EDGES

In the shop, a cotton buffing wheel replaces the strop. The rim of the buffer is rubbed with a tripoli abrasive compound and the final burr of the tool edge is cleanly removed by it. It does what the barber's strop did, but better and a thousand times faster.

Wearing down the "feather" of a freshly ground tool edge with such a buffer creates a microscopically rounded and smooth edge that will turn out to be the sharpest, smoothest, and strongest edge possible. Any future (microscopic) damage to that edge caused by prolonged use needs only this tripoli buffing to restore it to perfection.

Such occasional rebuffing may be the only resharpening required for a long time. When, in time, a dragging is felt during cutting it means that it is time to regrind the edge on *stone*. A feathered edge will, of course, result; and that will again call for the rapid removal of the burr with the tripoli-impregnated buffer as described.

No modern shop should be without a simple motor-driven buffing wheel if knifelike edges are to be sharpened at their best.

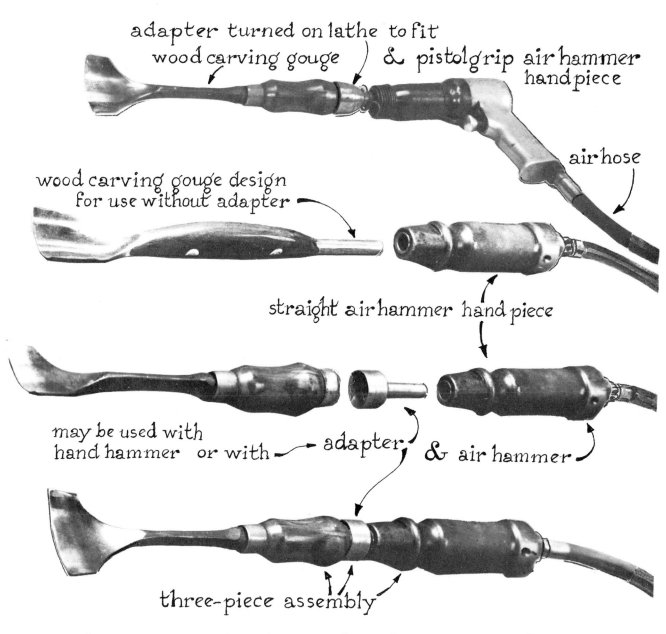

adapter turned on lathe to fit
wood carving gouge) & pistolgrip air hammer
handpiece

wood carving gouge design
for use without adapter

air hose

straight air hammer hand piece

may be used with
hand hammer   or with ➝ adapter & air hammer

three-piece assembly

woodcarving gouges forged from salvaged car leaf or coil springs.
adapters are turned on lathe from sections of scrapped car axles.
airhammer uses from 90 to 120 psi stored in a 100 gal. tank & a
1 to 2 hp motor driving one or two compressors

above hammer handpieces used without adapters for standard
stone carving tools, steelcutting tools

Engraver style wood-carving gouge shown on page 96 was used to carve this pipe in manzanita burl.

Engraving burins shown on page 93 cut designs on blocks of end-grain pearwood.

The Wave, by Alexander G. Weygers, engraved with burin shown on page 93 on end-grain pearwood.

Lifesize Indiana limestone carving of garden statue by Alexander G. Weygers made with tools forged from scrap steel.

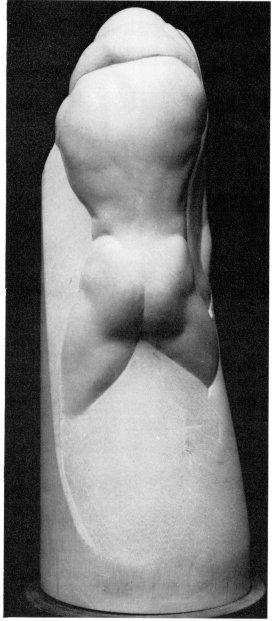

The Embrace, by Alexander G. Weygers, carved from salvaged lemonwood when orchards were destroyed to make way for housing developments. Tools used made from scrap steel of coil springs.

Glossary

ADAPTER. A driven instrument made to fit one type (size) of tool at one end and another type (size) at the other end.

AGITATOR. See *Paint Mixer*.

ALIGNMENT. In line with another element; not askew in relation to it.

ALLOY. A compound or fusion of two or more metals.

ANGLE IRON. Steel bars which have a cross section of an angle (usually 90°). The iron, in this term, is a holdover from the days before iron was made into steel. Now all angle iron is actually steel, either mild or high-carbon steel.

ANNEAL. To soften steel through slow cooling after enough heat has made the steel lose its brittleness.

APRON. In mechanics, an extended platform.

ARBOR. A wheel, axle, or shaft rotating in one or more bearings held by a frame that is bolted down.

AUGER. A wood drill, as a rule over 1 1/2 inches in diameter. (Also may refer to augers to drill holes in earth.)

BALL RACE. The parts of a ball bearing between which the balls "race."

BASTARD FILE. A file with teeth coarser than a smooth file and less coarse than a coarse file.

BEVEL. In cutting tools, the facet that has been ground at the cutting edge (inside and outside *bevels*).

BICK. A part that fits into an anvil's hardy hole and acts as a horn or *beck*.

BLANK. The rough shape of a tool before filing, grinding, etc. has prepared the tool for tempering and assembly with the handle.

BOSS. A locally raised part of steel.

BRITTLE QUENCH. See *Quench*.

BROACH. A boring tool, a reamer.

BUFFER. A cotton wheel used to polish surfaces.

BUFFING WHEEL. A motor-driven cotton wheel that rotates at high speed. A buffing compound rubbed into the cotton buffs (polishes) the steel held against the wheel.

BUNSEN BURNER. A gas burner with a single blue flame used in laboratories to heat liquids and objects.

BURIN. The cutting tool of an engraver.

BURR. A small rotary file, often used to take off a *burr* left on the edge of steel by previous cutting. A *burr* may also be the "feather-edge" left on a tool's cutting edge in the final step of sharpening the tool.

BUSH HAMMER. A tool with a hammer face having 9 or more raised points which, on impact, crush or pulverize the surface of stone. From the French *boucher:* to crush, to eat, to bite. The bush *tool* also has 9 or more raised points which, when hammered upon, crush or pulverize the surface of stone.

BUTTERFLY-CENTER. A lathe-center insert placed in headstock that has four sharp wings and a center pin which press into the wood that is to be turned on a wood lathe.

CAP SCREW (OR TAP-BOLT). A bolt (without its nut) screwed into a threaded hole of one part, to hold another part clamped onto the first.

CAPE CHISEL. A narrow chisel that cuts deep grooves, specifically key slots, in steel.

CARBIDE-TIP. An extremely hard tip soldered on to the end of a regular high-carbon steel bar used to turn wood or steel on a lathe.

CARRIAGE BOLT. A bolt which ties together wooden members in structures. It has a square section under the head to keep the bolt from turning.

CASE HARDENING. The process of applying a skin-deep hardness to the outer surface of mild steel in a forge fire.

CENTER-PUNCH. Tool used to make a "center" mark for locations to be drilled, or to mark off pattern outlines on steel.

CHASING TOOLS. Tools used to make marks (raised or depressed) in metal surfaces to create texture.

CHECKING (of wood). The splitting of wood during drying.

CHISEL. A metal tool with a blade having a sharp-edged end; used for cutting wood, stone, metal, or other material.

CHISEL. CARPENTER'S WOOD. A flat chisel for cutting wood.

CHISEL, COLD. A chisel that may be used on *cold* annealed steel to cut it.

CHISEL, HOT. A chisel used to cut *yellow hot* steel. The steel is cut with the hot chisel on the soft anvil table or a mild-steel plate placed over the hard anvil face. The chisel is either a hand-held long cold chisel or a sturdy chisel head fastened to a long wooden stem.

CHUCK. A clamp screwed on a rotating shaft to fasten drills, small grinders, etc.

CLAW. A multiple-toothed stonecarving tool used to refine the rough texture left by the one-point tool.

COEFFICIENT OF CONDUCTIVITY. A number that indicates the degree of speed at which heat is conducted from one spot to the next in a type of steel.

COIL SPRINGS. Springs made of long, high-carbon steel rods that are wound hot around a bar and afterward tempered the hardness for which such springs are designed.

COKE. The substance fresh coal becomes after heat has driven out all elements that give off smoke and yellow flame. Coke resembles charcoal in that it gives off a blue flame and lights easily.

COLLAR. A steel ring, often mounted on a shaft with a set screw.

CONDUIT PIPE. Galvanized steel pipe through which electricians install electric wires.

COUNTERSINK. A cone-shaped, large *drill bit* used to bevel the edge of a sharp-edged cylindrical hole left by a smaller drill; a shallow cylindrical depression around a hole, larger than the hole in diameter.

CUTOFF WHEEL. A thin abrasive wheel that cuts steel too hard to cut with a hacksaw.

109

DIE. A two-part mold (male and female) used for making and reproducing a form one or more times. The material is held between the dies that are then forced together to produce the form or shape that the dies have at their contacting planes. Dies are used strictly to mass-produce articles or to make an article that is too complicated to make easily by hand. (Also, a matrix.)

DOG. A tool clamped on the workpiece to engage the lathe headstock so that the workpiece can turn.

DOWEL (STEEL). A locking-pin that holds parts and keeps them from shifting their positions.

DRAWING OUT STEEL. *Stretching* steel, making it longer or wider or

DRAWING TEMPER COLOR. Reheating brittle-quenched steel that has been polished to see the oxidation color spectrum (temper colors) clearly. Once this color spectrum appears and the wanted color, which corresponds to its *hardness*, has been "drawn," the tool is quenched.

both. The opposite is to upset steel, making it thicker and/or shorter.

DRESSER. A tool that cuts or wears down the surface of grindstones.

DRESSING. Making an inaccurate grinding wheel accurate with a dresser by wearing the wheel surface down to exact shape.

DRIFT. A tapered steel pin which is driven into a hole in stone to split it. Another use is to pull together two slightly unmatched holes in two plates to align them perfectly.

DRILL BIT. Could be called a *drill*, but generally this term refers to a local *bit* at end of a plain drill rod. Such bits may be of varied designs to meet various drilling problems.

DRILL PRESS. A machine for drilling holes in metal or other material.

EMBOSS. To raise steel locally with bosses. The *boss* is a form of die which, pressed or hammered into the steel plate from one side, raises the steel surface on the other side of the sheet.

EYEBOLT. A bolt which has a hole in a round, flattened end instead of the hexagon, or round, or square-bolt head.

FACE. Generally refers to a flat surface on the sides or top of a tool or machine part: an anvil face, side-face, the face of a disc, "to face" a surface, when grinding, milling, and cutting steel surfaces.

FERRULE. A metal ring, cap, or tube-section placed on the end of a handle to keep it from splitting.

FIREBRICK. A brick which withstands high temperatures as in brick-lined kilns and fireplaces.

FIRECLAY. A clay which will not crack when fired.

FLANGE. A projecting rim; *also*, a plate to close a pipe opening.

FLASH FIRE. A fire that starts suddenly when an inflammable liquid reaches a heat corresponding to its "flash" point, setting the liquid aflame.

FLATTER. A tool shaped like a hammer head but with an accurate, square, flat face at one end and a crowned end at the other that can be struck with a heavy hammer. The flatter's face, placed on a heated inaccurate flat section of a workpiece lying on the anvil, can flatten it out accurately.

FORGE. A furnace in which steel is heated.

FREEZING. The bonding together of two clamped-together steel parts that have corroded or have been forcefully locked together. To break this bond is a frequent chore when taking rusted machinery apart.

FULLER. A blacksmith's tool that fits in the hardy hole of the anvil (bottom fuller), or is fastened on a long wooden stem (top fuller) in order to groove steel, draw it out, or "set" rounded corners. Comes in various sizes.

GAUGE. A specific size in reference to steel sheet or bar thickness, nail size, etc.

GRINDING POINTS. Miniature high-speed rotary grindstones.

HACKSAW. A hand saw with narrow blade set in metal frame, used to cut metal.

HARDY. An anvil insert that acts as a cutter of hot steel. Also called hardies are hardy-type tools that fit in the hardy hole, but have other special names, as a rule, i.e., *fullers*.

HARDY HOLE. The square hole in the anvil that the hardy fits into.

HEADING PLATE. A thick, flat piece of steel with a slightly tapered hole in the middle which receives a rod that has been upset at the end. The hot end can then be hammered into a head.

HEADSTOCK. The rotating driver end of a lathe.

HEAT. The period that the hot steel, removed from the fire, maintains its forging heat.

HEATING. The period of heating the steel.

HEAT TREATING. The process of *tempering* steel for a specific hardness; can also refer to treating steel to bring about a specific softness.

HIGH-CARBON STEEL. A temperable steel, primarily used to harden such steels for specific hardness in the process called "tempering." In industry, steel of over 0.2% carbon.

HOLD-DOWN OR HOLD-FAST. A contrivance for holding the heated workpiece to be forged when the smith needs both hands free to manipulate his tools. One end of the hold-down is rammed into the anvil's hardy or pritchel hole so that its other end will hold down (or hold fast) the workpiece.

HOLLOW GRIND. To grind the bevel of a cutting tool concave.

HONING. Grinding a steel surface with a *honing stone*. This stone leaves an almost-polished surface.

HP (HORSEPOWER). A unit of power, used in stating the power required to drive machinery.

JIG. A device which acts as as guide to accurately machine-file, fold, bend, or form a workpiece. This is used if lack of skill handicaps the worker in making the workpiece. Such jigs guide him and also save time in mass production of tools.

KEEPER. The part of a door latch through which the latch bolt slides.

LAPPING. An abrasive action in which a grinding compound is used between two surfaces that, when held pressed together in movement, grind themselves into one another.

LATHE. A machine for shaping articles which causes them to revolve while acted upon by a cutting tool.

LEAFSPRING. A spring with an oblong cross section and a sufficient length to act as a spring. Automobiles as a rule use such springs singly or in graduated layers to suspend the car body over the axles.

LOW-CARBON STEEL. A steel that is not temperable, which contains less then 0.2% carbon.

MALL. A larger hammer with wooden head, sometimes steel-weighted, used to drive stakes in the ground.

MALLEABLE. Capable of being shaped or worked by hammering, etc.

MALLET. A wooden hammer-head on a short handle used to hammer on wood-carving gouges. Sometimes the mallet head is made of rawhide or plastic or hard rubber.

MANDREL. A bar inserted in the workpiece to shape, hold, or grind it, as in a lathe.

MATRIX. A female die in which a malleable substance may be formed by pressing to fill it. A cavity in which anything is formed or cast.

MILD STEEL. A low-carbon steel. It is not temperable.

MILLING CUTTER. See *Seating Cutter*.

MORSE TAPER. A type of taper, named after its inventor, Mr. Morse, that holds fast to its seating in a clutch-like action without freezing to its surface and can be knocked loose easily when required.

NAIL SET. A tool resembling a center-punch but with a hardened, cup-shaped end instead of a ground point. This cup-shaped end, placed on the nail head center, keeps the tool from slipping sideways while "setting" the nail.

OFFSET. The step down (or up) in a bar or plate from its original alignment into another alignment, as a rule, parallel with it.

ONE-POINT TOOL. The basic stonecarving tool that "chips" stone in the first roughing-out action of stonecarving.

OXIDATION COLOR SPECTRUM. The color spectrum that results from the oxidation of cold steel as it gradually gets hot. The polished metal sheen shows the colors as clearly as the color spectrum in rainbows.

PACKING. Compacting a high-carbon steel to improve its quality by striking with heavy hammerblows when the steel is at cherry red heat.

PAINT MIXER (AGITATOR). A rod with a crooked end which, rotated in the paint, mixes it.

PATINA. The colored oxidation on metal surfaces. It results during the process of tempering the metal. (On bronze and many other metals, a patina comes about after long exposure to oxygen of the air and chemicals.)

PEARL GRAY. A typical file color. When high-carbon steel emerges from a quench, pearl gray indicates "file hardness."

PEEN END. A hammer with a wedge-shaped, round-edged end or a half-sphere ball end used to stretch steel by indentation. A *cross peen* hammer has the rounded edge of the peen at 90° to the hammer stem.

PILLOW. In mechanics, a supporting block that makes up the lower half of a split bearing.

PINION. A small gear that drives, or is driven by, a larger gear.

PRITCHEL HOLE. The round hole next to the square hardy hole in the anvil.

PUSH-ROD. The rod in an engine which "pushes" a valve to open the cylinder for the intake or expulsion of its gases.

QUENCH. To cool hot steel in a liquid. *Brittle quenching* is the act of cooling high-carbon steel at its critical heat at its fastest so that it will emerge brittle-hard.

QUENCHING BATH. The liquid into which the hot steel is dipped or immersed to cool it.

RASP. A coarse file used mostly to grate or tear softer materials such as wood, horn, plaster of Paris, and soft stones that are not abrasive.

RELIEF. A projection of a design or figure upward from a plane surface.

REPOUSSÉ. A raised surface on a flat plane achieved by pushing out from below a sheet the portions to be raised.

RHEOSTAT. An instrument which may be adjusted to let more, or less, electric current pass, for instance, to regulate the speed of an electric motor or to dim or brighten a light bulb.

ROUT. To cut or scoop out material with a router tool.

SADDLE. A rounded piece of steel on which to form another piece in its shape.

SCRIBE. A sharp-pointed steel marking pin used to scratch a line on to a workpiece.

SEATING CUTTER. Tool used to cut a *seat* in a part onto which another part fits exactly. The cutting also may be called *milling*, and the cutter then would be a *milling cutter*.

SET HAMMER. A hammer head fastened on a long wooden stem resembling a flatter. Placed on a partly formed section of a workpiece, it *sets* it into its final position when a regular hammer delivers a blow on it.

SET SCREW. A screw that clamps or *sets* one part onto another part.

SHANK. The part of a tool between tang and blade.

SHIM. A piece of thin material used to fill a space.

SHOULDER. In craft usage, an abrupt wider or thicker dimension in rod or shaft against which another part rests.

SLAG. A melted mix of non-combustible matter in coal. It lumps together.

SLEDGE. A heavy (6-pound or more) hammer on a long stem, used by the blacksmith's helper using both his hands, for heavy hammering of heavy steel.

SLEDGING. Striking with a sledge hammer.

SLEEVE. In bearings, the bushing; a precisely honed bronze tube that fits the shaft it bears.

SOCKET. An open part into which another part fits.

SPECTRUM. A division of colors occurring on the shiny part of steel when it is heated for tempering; similar to the rainbow colors seen through a prism.

SPRING STEEL. A high-carbon steel tempered so that it will act as a spring.

STEEL PLATE. Refers to flat sheets of steel thicker than 3/16 of an inch. It is optional at what thickness or thinness metal may be called sheet metal. Example: boilers are made of plate steel; stovepipes are made of sheet metal.

STEEL STOCK. The supply of steel from which an item is selected to forge, or machine, or grind the workpiece to be made.

STEP PULLEY. A ratio-increasing multiple pulley.

STROPPING. The final step in sharpening a cutting edge on a leather strop.

STUB SHAFT. A short, stubby shaft.

SWAGE. The "saddle" that is grooved to form steel and fits into the anvil's hardy hole (bottom swage), and a similar tool, fastened to a long wooden stem, placed *over* steel to form it (top swage).

TAILSTOCK. The center pin in the stationary end of the lathe that holds the rotating metal, wood or other material between the two lathe centers.

TANG. The part of the tool blank that is locked into the tool handle.

TEMPERABLE STEEL. A steel of a higher than 0.2% carbon quality which can be *tempered*.

TEMPERING. In forging metal, the process to arrive at a specific hardness of high-carbon steel.

TEMPLATE. A pattern, often made from cardboard or sheet metal, to serve as a model, the outline of which is scribed on the steel to be cut.

TINSNIPS. Sturdy, short-bladed shears that cut sheet metal.

TOOL REST (OR TOOL POST). As a rule, those parts on machines onto which a tool is held down firmly to be ground down. Also may refer to the clamp on a machine to hold a cutting tool.

TRIP-HAMMER. A mechanical hammer that is activated by tripping with the foot.

TRIPOLI. An abrasive-impregnated wax compound that, when rubbed into a rotating cotton buffing wheel, acts as the finest steel polisher.

UPSETTING. The process of making a piece of steel shorter and thicker.

VEINING TOOL. A V-shaped gouge that cuts V grooves referred to as "veins."

VISE. A two-jawed screw clamp bolted to the workbench to hold things steady while being worked.

VISEGRIP PLIERS. Self-locking pliers.

WELD. To fuse metals together under heat.

WROUGHT IRON. Iron that has been worked in a "puddling" process to purify it. It contains no carbon and is least subject to rusting. It is rarely used today, and hence not found in scrap piles. It can be welded easily and will not burn during melting as does steel.

On the front cover
TOP PICTURE:

1. scrap steel discs 5/16 inch thick
2. trip-hammer's anvil inset
3. disc shaped into cup between insets
4. trip-hammer's hammer inset
5. cup has been flanged
6. ball heads of various diameters
7. flanged cups hammered out on trip-hammer with 6
8. candlestick made from a car engine cam shaft section; candle drip basin, base turned from 3; candle socket as in 21
9. cooking ladle or fry cup on handle made from 3
10. cup with flanged "toe holds" for ball head to forge rosette leaves
11. triple popover fry cup on handle
12. scrap car axle cam shaft converted into candlestick similar to 8
13. candlestick
14. hand-held punch to ram a tube section into a cone die to taper the tube end
15. two wood-carving gouges that have cup shoulders forged from 20 and 22
16. same as 14
17. set of dies, which form hand-hammered 20 and 22
18. wood lathe jig, which turns burin handles
19. engine valve grinding jig based on reverse lathe principle
20. wood-carving tool blank with large shoulder to be forged into a shoulder-cup combination
21. candle socket with taper end shaped in the anvil die
22. wood-carving tool blank with medium shoulder
23. reverse lathe unit with one adjustable sliding center to accommodate various sizes handle stock, to turn tool handles that fit standard ferrule sizes

BOTTOM PICTURE:

1. recycled shovel—curved handle is made of fruitwood
2. charcoal brazier made of car headlight and wheel hubcap
3. charcoal tongs
4. charcoal scoop
5.–15. pattern punches to cut designs in sheet metal
16. large wood-carving gouge made from a plow disc
17.–18. wood-carving gouges designed for sculpture carving
19. small chisels for cutting relief medallions in steel
20. wood-cutting jig to shape wood handle ends
21. bowl-carving gouge used to cut wooden bowls
22.–27. pattern punches to cut designs in sheet metal
28. bowl-carving gouge
29. sample design punched out of sheet metal with pattern punches
30. stone-carving tools and mild steel hammer for sculpturing
31. wood-carving gouges used with adapter in air hammers
32. wood-carving gouges that fit air hammer handpieces without an adapter
33. air hammer with rubber hose muffler, and a wood-carving tool adapter
34. air hammer handpiece with pistol grip and rubber muffler and an inserted wood-carving gouge adapter